WHORES, WARS
AND WASTE

WHORES, WARS AND WASTE

ANTICS OF THE MODERN BRITISH ARMY

Richard T. Sharpe

JANUS PUBLISHING COMPANY
London, England

First published in Great Britain 2002
by Janus Publishing Company Ltd,
76 Great Titchfield Street,
London W1P 7AF

www.januspublishing.co.uk

British Library Cataloguing-in-Publication Data.
A catalogue record for this book
is available from the British Library.

ISBN 1 85756 506 1

Typeset in 10pt Baskerville

Cover Design Hamish Cooper

Printed and bound in Great Britain

Contents

'I suggest two maxims for successful command. The first
is that it must be exercised in a relaxed manner at all
levels, for only a happy unit will be successful and in a
happy unit no one can be afraid of his seniors.
This must be accompanied by the utmost attention to
detail in order to keep things up to the mark.'
Brigadier Sir Martin Lindsay of Downhill CBE DSO

'If, when you are appointed to command a battalion, you
are worried about how to exercise that command then
you should not have been appointed in the first place
experience should have prepared you.
We all know and can assess physical risks. However, the
successful commander must also take risks in the field of
decision making and it is in this principle that so many
commanders fail.'
Major General Peter de la Billiere DSO MC

'Whoever does not have the stomach for this fight, let
him depart. We few, we happy few, we band of brothers;
for whoever has shed his blood with me shall be my
brother.'
William Shakespeare's Henry V

A Note on Security

All the stories in this book are true. In nearly all cases I was there and personally witnessed them. Those that are hearsay have been recounted to me by at least two individuals who were there at the time and will be annotated as such.

To protect the identity of personnel concerned, some of the details have been obscured and military formations and specific locations are not identified for obvious security reasons.

It is not my intention to try to make any individuals or organisations appear incompetent. They were, at worst, perhaps confused or they misunderstood the ground rules. Nevertherless, some were obviously in the wrong place at the wrong time and some should never have been in the given situation.

In many cases people were just being their true and natural selves.

Introduction

My army service started in early 1970 and spanned a total of 24 years and 97 days. During that time I was fortunate enough to work with, and in, a wide and varied assortment of military organisations, units, regiments and corps. These ranged from rear echelon Service Support Corps to front line Special Forces units, and even the Territorial Army. I had the privilege of meeting royalty, ministers of state and high-ranking service officers, and finally retired into civilian life after being the RSM* of two units.

Throughout these years I experienced many interesting and memorable moments, which when recounted to others nearly always prompted them to say, "you should write a book". Well, here it is.

Some of the stories in this book are funny and some are sad. Some will show how the so-called 'modern professional British Army' has not progressed as far as many senior people, in both the political and military arenas, would have the general public believe. In some cases the very word 'professional' may need reviewing.

The book is not intended as either an autobiographical or a chronological historical record of my military career but is a collection of incidents that occurred during those 24 years 97 days. I have tried not to tell any actual war stories as I believe that these are best recounted by military historians and those who have access to the official facts and figures.

To truly appreciate these accounts you should understand the way

---

*I held the rank of Warrant Officer Class One, which is the highest non-commissioned rank attainable in the British Army and is usually the Senior Warrant Officer in any unit.

the British Army really works. First it is made up of many thousands of volunteers from all age groups (teens to pensioners), from a wide and diverse variety of backgrounds.[†] You will find officers with five O-level GCEs and a private with a degree or two. You have all sexualities and genders in both support and front-line occupations, along with all ethnic and religious persuasions.

The Army is made up of both committed professionals who make the Army their lives and those who join purely for socio-economic reasons. A number join just to get away from abusive parents or dismal family situations, some are intent on learning a trade, some join under the mistaken impression that they will see the world and others join simply because they are totally unsuitable for employment elsewhere.[‡] Even today people still enlist because they are led to believe that they have a family tradition to maintain and uphold. To put it rather simply, the British Army is made up of a hotchpotch of individuals, all working for their own benefit and gain, whilst displaying a unified and collective image.

[†]This may have changed by the time this book goes to press, as there are consistent rumours about the compulsory call up of Territorial Army personnel to counter the current overstretch and overcommitment of the Regular Army.

[‡]During the period of my service most of our remaining permanent overseas posts were closed down or drastically reduced, e.g. Hong Kong, Belize, Canada, Gibraltar, Germany, to name a few. However, with the UK's continuing commitment to support NATO and the United Nations in their policing of world troublespots, British servicemen and women are still able to travel to some far-off places. Even if, once there, they are not allowed out of barracks at night to mix freely with the local population and see much of the country they are occupying.

Boys' Service

When I joined the Army in 1970 I was fifteen and a half years old and in those days you could enlist into the Boys' Service.

This meant you attended a boarding-type establishment called either a Junior Leaders' Regiment or an Army Apprentice College. These were run by the Army along squadron or company lines, where the main objectives were to increase your general educational standards, provide you with basic army training and ultimately to prepare you for a long and illustrious military career.

You usually remained in Boys' Service until you reached seventeen and a half, or at the end of that term, and then you transferred to Men's Service and the real Army.

Electrified Lockers

One boy soldier I remember was getting annoyed with the amount of petty pilfering going on from his locker. The lockers were all metal and approximately 6ft tall, 4ft wide and 2ft 6ins deep. You had one each and had to keep all your personal and military possessions in them.

Each boy in the barrack room had a bed space in which he had a metal-framed bed and a metal bedside cabinet, a small rug, a metal-framed chair and his metal locker.

This particular boy soldier decided that enough was enough and it was time for drastic action. He rigged up the metal locker so that it was permanently connected to the mains electricity supply. His idea was that anyone attempting to steal his kit would receive such a shock that they wouldn't do it again.

1

The only giveaway was that the locker used to glow in the dark.

Smoking Cabinet

The metal lockers also had one non-military use for us boys. We could empty them and use them for terrifying or bullying another boy if he upset someone.

To do this we would remove the contents of the locker and make the victim stand or kneel, depending on how big he was, in the half of the locker used for hanging uniform or civilian clothes. We would then close the door on that side, securing it with a pencil or matchsticks. While that door was sealed using ducting or insulating tape, old newspapers would be torn up and placed in the drawer on the other side of the locker. These would then be set alight and the other door closed and sealed.

It became a fine art to know how long to leave the locker sealed before you had to let the hostage out. I must admit that on some occasions the injured party would emerge in a very poor and traumatised state.

Chasing Cars

I recall one rather senior boy soldier who developed a morbid fascination with road traffic accidents.

He would lie in his bed at night listening to a radio receiver tuned to the local emergency frequencies. When he heard a call for either an ambulance or fire engine to anywhere near our camp, he would jump out of bed, put on his tracksuit and disappear to the scene of the accident on his motor scooter. Returning that night only to bore all the other boys in the barrack room with the gory details of the event.[1]

Young Infatuations

During my time as a boy soldier I was made an NCO in charge of one of the barrack rooms.[2] At the start of a new term I had some new recruits to look after. One lad was acutely homesick and would cry himself to sleep each night. Initially this was to the amusement of the

2

other boys but finally became a nuisance. So the poor lad had to endure a ritual beating each night to ensure that he had something worthwhile to cry about.

On a morning inspection it was noted that he had stuck several small posters to the inside of his locker (you were not permitted to stick them on the walls). The posters were of a dance group that performed regularly on television and were considered rather raunchy, even bordering on erotic. They were idealised by nearly every heterosexual member of the unit.

Tackled about these, the lad told us that he actually knew one of the girls. As he was a fifteen-year-old spotty-faced thing, first time away from home and definitely a virgin, this was taken as total rubbish, even an attempt to curry favour with his mentors. In true and time-honoured fashion, he was ceremoniously beaten.

However, to our amazement, two of the dance group did turn up to see this lad on his end of term Passing-In Parade and departed, after the parade, in the same car as him when he went off on his leave. We never saw him again!

Flagpoles and Skeletons

The night prior to a winter Passing-Out Parade for the Men's Service recruits, with whom we shared the camp, some of our lads decided to play a small prank on them. After lights-out two lads were sent off to the Education Centre, while others sneaked off across the Parade Square.

Next morning, with less than one hour before the parade was to start, we watched in fits of helpless laughter as one of the Recruit Instructors finally noticed our joke. We had, with much effort and skill, lowered the main flagpole just behind the saluting base and secured an anatomical skeleton to the top. When the pole was returned upright it was made impossible to lower it again by the liberal use of fast-action glue.

To say that the Depot RSM was not impressed was a major under-statement. With parents and dignitaries watching, the local fire brigade was called to cut the offending item down. However, the full blame fell on the recruits themselves as we had cannily used our already impressive tactical training and placed footprints in the snow going to and from their barrack room windows and doors on to the Parade Square.

Seaside Stories

Upon his return from Easter leave one lad was asked if he had had a good time. Renowned for his supposed sexual exploits, Pete slowly described, with full and intimate details, a recent conquest he had while walking along the seafront of his home town one morning.

This caused several lads to go weak at the knees with pure envy and some had to resort to self-satisfaction to overcome the full effect of Pete's endeavours.

As he finished and set about putting his civvies away into his locker, one of the boys asked if he had managed to sneak any porno books into the camp. Yes, of course he had and he duly handed one over. Not ten minutes passed before the lad was back and calling Pete all the names under the sun.

Asked what the problem was, he produced the said magazine and read a letter to the editor. It went something like this:

'Last week as I walked along the beach of my seafront town I encountered a blonde, big - breasted young lady as she emerged from swimming in the sea. She smiled, I smiled'... and the rest was as told by Pete.

Punishment for this was a freezing cold bath, scrubbing with toilet brushes and scouring powder and a liberal application of after shave to his private parts.

Sexual Awareness

In any close environment involving young adolescents, whether it is the Forces or public schools, sexual awareness is always an issue that will rear its head. Therefore, homosexual experiences were had by most and some continued this orientation once they reached maturity and transferred to Men's Service.

After lights - out and bed - check were complete, all sorts of activities would occur.[3] Whole barrack rooms would engage in wanking

4

competitions where the first to climax won a small pot of money. The winners from each barrack room would be matched against the winner from another room, with all the room occupants sitting around watching.

It was also not unknown for boy soldiers who had been granted NCO status and given their own bunks to invite other boys in for a late night tryst. Some boys became very close indeed and it was well known among the remaining lads (and to some of the Men's Service SNCOs, Warrant Officers and officers that supervised the Boys' Service) that something was going on.

Just before my time in Boys' Service, a sergeant major at the unit was severely disciplined for having rather dubious relations with some of the lads, under the guise of adventure training and camping trips during hobbies weekends.[4]

One of the retired officers on the staff, employed to teach educational subjects, was also a member of the Magic Circle. He was also well known for his sexual leanings but nevertheless was still allowed to invite individual Boy Soldiers back to his home, where he entertained them (and no doubt himself) with his 'magical tricks'.

Senior Boys' Night Out

One of the traditions at the end of each term, and there were three a year, was that the senior boys were treated to a night out. This took the form of a psuedo-regimental dinner at a local hotel and was the only time us Boy Soldiers were 'officially' permitted to consume alcohol.

It was also a social function that instilled fear into the junior soldiers. The seniors would return to the camp inebriated and in a rowdy mood, this would inevitably lead to fights and the settling of old scores (most of the officers and instructors would be drunk too).

I well remember one senior boy going into a barrack room occupied by our newest recruits just before he departed for a Senior Boys' Night Out. He gathered the recruits around and informed them that when he returned he would come back drunk and beat up each and every one of them. The fifteen-year-olds had experienced this lad's fighting prowess before and knew that he, at nearly eighteen years

5

old, was physically bigger and stronger than they were. However, the older lad gave them an alternative. If they stood in their respective bed spaces and allowed him to thump them only once, he promised not to return later.

As good recruits they believed him and he went round the barrack room hitting each one in turn. He finally departed for the dinner as the odd nose was put back, some blood spilt, teeth damaged and the odd bruised eye bathed in iced water

Just after midnight the bus returned and disgorged the thirty or so drunken senior boys who staggered into the barracks. Those left in the camp pretended to be asleep, as the drunks roamed the accommodation looking for their victims. The senior boy who had promised to be kind and considerate upon his return sorted out a few other problems before bursting into the barrack room in which the recruits slept. He systematically visited every bed space, inflicting more pain and agony on each boy. The new recruits had learnt one basic rule of army life - Never believe anything you are told by anyone.

Heavy Sleeper.

One of the boys who slept in a barrack room on the third floor of our accommodation block was well renowned for his heavy sleeping, his inability to get up in the mornings and for his snoring. So, one night a fiendish plot was hatched to humiliate the said soldier.

Once he was well asleep, he was gently picked up on his mattress and carried out of the barrack room, down the stairs and outside the accommodation. At the same time, the window next to his bed space was opened and his bed frame pushed out, where it hit the ground and crumpled slightly. The still snoring lad was carefully placed across the frame as if he had fallen with the bed.

Later that night the prowler guard found him and the look of shock horror on his face when they finally woke him was reported to be an absolute treat. After that the lad insisted on bed space nowhere near a window and became a much lighter sleeper. The snoring also stopped.

Crucifixion

If one of the new recruits or a junior Boy Soldier upset a Boy's Service NCO, he could be treated to the unofficial punishment of 'crucifixion'. He would be made to put on his service issue combat jacket and do all the zips and buttons up. A broom handle would then be pushed up one sleeve, across the back of the jacket and down the other sleeve.[5] The victim would then be manhandled until the ends of the broom were sitting between the tops of two adjacent lockers and his feet were off the floor.

The length of time he had to suffer this depended on whom he had upset and what he had actually done. While hanging there he could also be subjected to further forms of abuse, both mental and physical, i.e. he could have his genitals liberally doused in aftershave or strips of toilet tissue inserted into his rectum and then set on fire.

Hot Iron Treatment

Another form of punishment for anyone transgressing the unwritten rules of Boys' Service was for them to be subjected to the Hot Iron Treatment. This was a highly entertaining pastime, unless you were the victim of course, and consisted of holding the accused down on a bed, removing his shirt or vest, while displaying a very hot steam iron, before his eyes.

His eyes were then covered and a big commotion was made of his offence, his character, and what the punishment was going to consist of. Once all the hype was complete the hot iron would be moved ever closer to his bare chest. The victim would squirm, scream, and really believe that the steam iron was about to be placed on his skin. Occasionally steam would be expelled from the iron and this would singe the boy's chest.

At the very last moment the hot iron would be replaced with a cold metal mess tin and quickly pressed down onto his chest.

Down the Pub

As I neared the end of my time in Boys' Service we were paid Men's

Service wages (after reaching seventeen and a half years of age). We were rich compared to the rest and this allowed us a few privileges. One was being able to afford to sneak off to the local pubs for a beer. So once a fortnight three of us booked out and headed across the Army Training Area behind camp to a small country pub.

We were sure the landlady knew who we were and where we came from but as long as we sat in the lounge and didn't cause any problems we were always made welcome. She even produced plates of sandwiches for us occasionally.

One night as we sat by the open fire drinking the pure nectar of illegal ale, we were horrified to see one of our military instructors walk in with a lady. Once he noticed us he indicated that one of us should meet him in the toilets and we sheepishly obeyed. We assumed that this was to start the inevitable disciplinary action that should surely follow our flagrant breach of the rules.

After fifteen minutes, or what seemed like a lifetime, they returned from the toilets. Not much had been said, except that we were to immediately drink up and leave, and to say nothing at all about the incident. It turned out that the lady with the instructor was not his wife.

Foot Inspection

As the Boys' Service Sergeant in charge of my company it was my responsibility to carry out the morning inspection on certain days of the week. On this occasion I called my two corporals together just prior to the inspection and informed them that I would be carrying out a foot inspection that morning. They then went off to inform the lance corporals in charge of the individual barrack rooms.

It was common practice to start at Room One and work your way numerically to the last one. So this morning I started at Room One and the inspection went reasonably well. All personnel to be inspected had removed their boots and socks and were standing to attention, in their respective bed spaces. However, on leaving Room One I decided to rush down to Room Three and try to catch them off guard.

On entering, the lance corporal in charge called the room to attention but some of the individuals were not ready. In fact, I caught one lad sitting on his bed, cleaning between his toes with a wet finger, which he licked clean in between each attempt. This nearly made me vomit so the inspection was halted while the offender was stripped naked and escorted to the showers, where he was unceremoniously plunged under a cold shower and scrubbed with a stiff yard brush and scouring powder.

Swimming v. Sports

Tuesday and Thursday afternoons were spent in the pursuit of sporting excellence. But before you could advance to the playing fields you had to pass the standard Military Swimming Test. This meant jumping into the pool, treading water for two minutes and then swimming (breast stroke only) one hundred yards.

The swimmers departed for the pool just after lunch and were the first group to finish and return to barracks. I never failed to be amused at the number of strong and capable swimmers who would regularly fail the swimming test by either getting cramp, partial drowning or by grabbing hold of the side of the pool in sheer exhaustion, rather than being forced to play rugby, football, cricket, or being dispatched on the ubiquitous cross-country run.

Church Parades

On a regular basis all the Boy Soldiers had to dress up in their best civilian clothes and march off to Sunday church services. As a new recruit I went to the Anglican church, which was at the far end of the camp, only to note that over the weeks the number of boys attending noticeably reduced. Perplexed about this, I asked one of the senior boys how or why this was occurring.

It transpired that several had seen the light and had converted to Catholicism. Not for any religious reason I must add, but purely on the grounds that the Catholic church was in the middle of the camp and its service was shorter than ours. This meant that they could get back to barracks earlier and could be first in the queue for lunch or the NAAFI.

Needless to say, I immediately applied to change my religion to Catholic and thereafter my Sundays were much improved.

General Military Service

When I left Boys' Service we were not required to attend Basic Recruit Training but were posted directly to units to begin our trade training. Trade training or, as it is called now, Special to Arms training, should form the main core of your military life and still remains one of the main reasons for personnel joining the Army. I always felt it really important that all service personnel gain a trade while they have the opportunity. This should be achieved as a priority over travel, money and promotion.

When I reached the illustrious and dizzy heights of Senior NCO and then Warrant Officer I made a point of explaining this to all new soldiers that came before me during their arrivals interview. There really isn't a great calling for ex-servicemen who can chew steel nails, jump out of iron birds, run twenty miles with a heavy pack on their backs and kill people.

Shot In The Arm

On posting into Men's Service from Boys' Service I thought life would be much better all round. How wrong I was.

I moved into accommodation that had been condemned over ten years before. I was allocated a bed space in a wooden Nissan hut that also housed another fifteen soldiers. We each had a metal locker for our possessions, a metal bedside cabinet, metal-framed bed, metal chair and small bedside rug. The toilets, baths and washbasins were a hundred yards away (there were no showers). The dining room was a Nissan hut and that was over a quarter of a mile away.[6]

Each room had a Junior NCO in charge (usually a corporal), who

11

lived in a bunk attached to the Nissan hut. Rooms were inspected daily by the Orderly Sergeant and at least weekly by the RSM.

After I had been there six weeks or so, I was rudely awoken one evening by someone sitting across my chest and punching me in the face. Evidently this soldier, a thirty-one-year old corporal, who lived in one of the other huts, had decided to visit my barrack room and vent off some of the beer he had consumed in the unit bar. As there were only two of us sleeping in the hut that night we were easy pickings for this older soldier. The remainder of the occupants were either on guard duty or out of barracks for one reason or other.

After we finally ejected the drunk we wandered off to the washrooms to inspect and repair the damage to our faces. While doing this another JNCO came in and was rather horrified to see us washing blood from our injuries. He inquired as to what had happened and left in a real rage, which was intensified when I told him who had carried out the assault. He evidently did not like the other NCO concerned.

Just after we got back to our barrack room the compassionate NCO came in. He was still obviously very annoyed at what the drunken NCO had done, but he stated that he had been to see him, had sorted him out and that he would not be a problem to us again. This intrigued both myself and the other soldier involved, so we went off to find our assailant. As we drew near to this NCO's bunk we could hear whimpering and wondered what had gone on between them. There was no answer to our knocks on the bunk door so we opened it and looked in.

The drunken corporal had obviously received some of his own medicine but the main cause of the whimpering was the fact that he was pinned to the wooden wall by a cross bow bolt that stuck out of his upper arm.

Military Discipline

British soldiers are subject to a whole host of rules and regulations. You are subject to the common law of the land in which you serve, be it the UK, Germany, the United States, or elsewhere in the world.[7] You are also subject to the provisions and Acts under the Manual of

Military Law. Mandatory edicts as laid down in Queen's Regulations for the Army and such things as AGAIs (Army General Administrative Instructions) will also have a profound effect on your life. Of course, Ministry of Defence, Command, District, Garrison and Unit Standing Orders, along with Unit Daily Part One Orders, all have to be adhered to.

Unlike civilian law it always appears that a soldier is guilty until proved innocent. Military discipline can be turned and twisted to suit any occasion, for example, when inspecting his troops, a sergeant asks a soldier why he looks like a sack of worms tied in the middle with a piece of string. If the man does not reply he could be charged with dumb insolence. On the other hand, had he replied, he could be charged with insubordination and, if all else fails, the sergeant could use section 69 of the Army Act 1955 which covers 'conduct to the prejudice of good order and military discipline'.

Death of the Goldfish

A concession we were granted by the RSM at one of our training units was that we were allowed to have a fish tank in our barrack room. This we stocked with goldfish and wrote up a roster for feeding them and cleaning their tank. These were our pride and joy, a minor piece of civilisation in an otherwise drab military environment.

One evening while we were out on the town one of my room-mates managed to remove an ornamental sword off the wall of one of the pubs. This instrument of amusement was carried back to the barracks where mock battles were acted out. As more beer and wine was consumed and the night drew on, the sword fencing got more daring. Broom handles, mops and the odd piece of furniture succumbed to the razor-sharp edge of the sword.

Finally, our attention drifted towards the fish tank. If pirates on the Spanish Main could fight man-eating fish then so could we.

Next morning we awoke, with heavy heads and delicate stomachs, the obvious effects of too much alcohol the night before. To our horror the room was awash with water and the walls and furniture covered in the remains of our beloved goldfish.

Beers for Breakfast

One of the units I was posted to for trade training had an NCO in charge of all the accommodation. However, this was no ordinary NCO. He had completed twenty-one years' loyal service to Queen and country, attaining the dizzy heights of Acting Lance Corporal. Brummie, as we called him, was the only non-tradesman I ever met in the British Army.[8]

His total area of responsibility was the Junior Ranks' accommodation. His duties included the allocation of bed spaces or bunks, issuing and receiving bedding, and the cleaning of toilets, ablutions and communal areas. He had to do these personally, as there were no civilian cleaners employed.

Not surprising then that Brummie was the butt of many people's merriment. He had just under a year to go for his full service pension and retirement into whatever he wanted to do for the rest of his life.

Brummie was well known within the unit as a pitiful alcoholic and could be seen most mornings cleaning his teeth with a bottle of beer in his hand. He stored crates of drink under his bed and would often be found in the afternoon, in his bunk, too drunk to stand.

Unfortunately the combination of military and medical neglect, compounded with the ridicule he received from all ranks, peaked just before his discharge date, when Brummie was found in his bunk dead from inhaling his own vomit.

It's Raining Indoors

While still a young soldier I had to share a barrack room with eleven others. One was a rather puerile Junior NCO attached to my unit from the Intelligence Corps, who seemed to do nothing with his spare time other than drink real ale and get fatter by the day. Another was an ex-Para, who was the unit Post NCO, and spent his time chasing other soldiers' wives and dodging letters from his ex-wife asking for maintenance payments. Each man had a fairly large bed space that included a couple of the ubiquitous army metal lockers, army metal-framed bed and the metal bedside cabinet. However, we were allowed to add to this with small items of our own. I had a small coffee table, which stood under a window with my small stereo system on it.

Into bed early one evening I was awoken by the sound of splashing water, which seemed to be close to my head. Had I left the window open and it had started to rain? No, standing not a foot away from me was a rather intoxicated, flatulent Intelligence Corps lance corporal who, in his drunken stupor, had taken to somnambulism and mistaken my coffee table for the urinal.

After diving out of bed and escorting the man back to his own bed space, I spent some time drying out my stereo and hoping that the thing would not explode the next time I switched it on. After getting back into bed and having just dropped off to sleep I was once again woken by unusual nocturnal sounds. This time it was the ex-Para postie beating the living daylights out of the Intelligence Corps NCO who had just urinated in the man's locker.

Vaults From Hell

During your Army service you will be sent on, or will volunteer for, a variety of training courses. These can be adventurous, trade or pro-motional-based and either in the UK or abroad. They will take up a goodly portion of your time when you are not off defending the realm or standing around knee-deep in freezing mud, usually at night, in some exotic location, such as Salisbury Plain, waiting for some faceless senior officer sitting in his cosy headquarters sipping tea trying to think of another pointless manoeuvre to send you on.

One of the courses I attended was to train NCOs to become Assistant Instructors of Physical Training: eighteen weeks of ten-hour days, five days a week, running, jumping and shouting while attempting to encourage your fellow students into feats of majestic athleticism.

We had one lad who had been sent on the course by his command-ing officer for some rather obscure reason. He was not at all interested in the ideals of the course, did not want to be away from his home base in Scotland and much preferred to be out with his pals drinking crates of beer.

As part of the course we had to pass a series of tests to progress to the next phase. One of these was a daring piece of gymnastics called a long thief vault. This called for the gymnast to run at a vaulting box, placed lengthways, launch off a beat-board and traverse the top of the box with legs together and at ninety degrees to his upright body, toes pointed, and smiling of course.

Unfortunately, our reluctant friend from north of the border did not have the guts to give his all and failed this test on at least three consecutive runs. The Staff Instructor from the Army Physical Training Corps decided that Jock must continue to practise this manoeuvre while we went on to the rope climbing test.

As we climbed and descended the ropes, toes pointed and with forced smiles on our faces, we could hear Jock charging around the gym, hitting the beat-board and occasionally bouncing off the front or sides of the vaulting box.

Suddenly it all went quiet from Jock's part of the gym. The Staff Instructor halted everything and looked around-no sign of Jock. Students were dispatched to all parts of the gym to hunt for him. Finally we heard a low muffled cry and upon approaching the vaulting box the cry got louder.

We found Jock inside the box with a dislocated shoulder and suffering concussion. He had at last plucked up the courage to have a full-blown go at the required vault. Running at the box full steam ahead, he had bounced off the beat-board but lifted his legs too late, caught his toes under the top lid of the box, lifted it and shot straight inside.

Bed Wetting

Another incident that happened during my training as an Assistant Physical Training Instructor concerned a trainee and a vast quantity of cider.

One of the trainees had the reputation as a drinker of some renown and would often be seen heading off to the bedding store first thing Monday morning to exchange his mattress after he had urinated on it, caused solely by poor bladder control while inebriated or, to use the military vernacular, 'while out of his tree'.

As I lived in the local area I decided one weekend to call upon the man and, with a few friends, go out for a beer or two to see if the stories about his drinking were correct. So at midday we turned up at his barrack block and found his room. He had a one-man bunk and was the only trainee left in barracks this weekend (apart from the trainees who formed the camp guard). As he did not answer our knocks on his bunk door, we opened it and looked in. The curtains were closed so we switched the lights on and were astonished to see that he was fully clothed lying on the bed. By the smell he had certainly urinated in the room and was in what appeared to be a deep drunken stupor.

To our utter amazement he had a small plastic barrel of cider on top of his bedside cabinet that was connected to his forearm by a medical intravenous drip set.

Back to the Depot

Having completed my Assistant Instructor's course in Physical Training, I was posted back to the training depot to take up an appointment in the gymnasium, or at least that was what it said on my posting order. Unfortunately, on my arrival I was informed that they only employed Army Physical Training Corps Instructors and not Assistant Instructors. I was further informed that I would actually be employed on the demonstration team based at the depot. This was not, as the name implies, a demonstration team in any form, nor was it a recruiting team, but a group of fifteen soldiers led by a sergeant, whose tasks included putting up tentage for sports days, waiting at tables on Officers' Mess dinner nights, acting as enemy on field exercises for promotion and recruit courses, plus the sweeping up of the ubiquitous leaves and painting of white lines. In a nutshell, we were the dogsbodies for the Depot.

As this was not the job that I was posted in to do, I discussed the situation with one of the senior sergeants on the depot headquarters staff. He advised me to put in a Redress of Grievance against my last commanding officer who had led me to believe I was going to the depot to work in the gymnasium. The HQ Chief Clerk spent hours with me going through the procedure and drafting the actual Redress. I then submitted it up through the chain of command and awaited some form of action.

Several months after the submission of my Redress of Grievance I was called into the HQ Company Commander's office to be told two important pieces of news. First, that my Redress was now being considered at 'the highest level' and I should hear their conclusion(s) in the next few weeks. Secondly, the commanding officer against whom I had redressed had been promoted to brigadier and was due to take up his new appointment in a month's time. He was to be the new commandant of the depot.

As a lowly lance corporal with just a few years' service I decided that it was in the best interests of my military career to cut and run. I withdrew the Redress and applied for a posting.

Nowt so Strange as Folk

As I languished at the depot I witnessed a strange event that still troubles me. At meal times I would sit with the rest of the demonstration team and one day a specific recruit was pointed out to me. It was explained that he was a touch weird and his behaviour was becoming noticed. So for the next few days we all watched him whenever he came into the dining hall. He queued up with the rest of his recruit intake but, as he approached the servery, he would start a religious blessing for all the food being served. Having taken his food and drink he would sit alone at a table and again bless the food before he started eating.

Then one day he failed to turn up for the evening meal and we asked his fellow recruits what had happened to him. We were informed that earlier that day they had all been interviewed by the officer responsible for allocating their trades and initial postings. When our eccentric, or weird, recruit was interviewed he was asked what trade he would like to take up. His answer mortified the officer when he explained that he was only interested in one particular trade. This trade did not require any formal educational qualifications yet our recruit had seven GCE Advanced level certificates to his name. Asked why he only wanted this trade, he further explained that before he joined the Army he was lying in bed one night when God appeared before him in a halo of brilliant light and had instructed him to enlist into the Army and to take up this trade as a way of helping mankind.

Prematurely terminating the interview, the officer placed a few

18

phone calls and the recruit was sent off to be examined by a military psychiatrist. For some reason we never saw that recruit again.

Room Inspections

One unit that I served in as a Junior NCO (lance corporal and corporal) had the honour of moving into brand new barracks. This had cost several million pounds and the hierarchy were determined to keep them looking nice and new for years to come; not that we were intent on smashing the place up of course. The accommodation was extremely good and each soldier had his own room with sink and fitted lockers. The major drawback from this was that our Squadron Sergeant Major (SSM) insisted on doing daily room inspections. All hell would break loose if marks were found on the walls, doors, or carpets.

One lad had a large fish tank installed in his room (it appears that fish tanks are popular with soldiers for some reason). This measured 3ft x 2ft x 2ft and was well set up, even had a little diver at the bottom along with a model of a sunken ship. Whatever the mathematic formula it did contain a few gallons of water, but after one inspection the SSM called the occupant to his office and told him to get rid of the tank as it was a fire hazard.

The same SSM called one of the unit's vehicle mechanics to his office after an accommodation inspection to inform him that he had too many pairs of shoes in his room and that in the SSM's opinion they constituted a physical hazard should the soldier have to evacuate the room in an emergency. The soldier was told to either get rid of some of the shoes or find alternative storage for them. Needless to say, the soldier did nothing about this and was called back to the SSM's office a week later and informed that he had been fined £10 for not complying with the shoe order.[9]

As he was leaving the SSM's office the Sergeant Major asked him if he would have a look at his private car, as there was some sort of problem with the engine. The mechanic agreed to do so, in his own time that evening, and told the SSM that it would cost £10 plus any parts.

Rugby Tackle

Sports will take up much of your in-barracks time. They are seen as character building, good for team spirit and regimental esprit de corps. From a soldier's point of view sports allow them to get away from the drudgery of daily barrack life and occasionally to let their well-trimmed hair down.

British Army sportsmen and women participate at all levels up to and including international level. They can be seen in all disciplines both as individuals and team members. The down side to this is that they generally have to forsake their military career to play at top levels of competition for sustained periods.

While I was, and still am, a great advocate of sports and fitness within the services, I saw some very promising military careers put on hold because a commanding officer insisted that a soldier, or officer, could not be spared to attend a course but had to represent the unit at a certain event or other. In some cases this meant soldiers falling behind their peers in both trade and rank. This would also mean a loss in the one great thing that motivates most service personnel money.

I used to enjoy my Wednesday afternoon rugby games. We played against a varied and mixed level of teams but always played hard and tried to win at all costs. This attitude was instilled into us by our Second-in-Command (2i/c) who played with us and acted as coach, trainer and social manager. He was, unfortunately, also prone to overdoing things on occasions.

Having been sent off in a previous match for hitting the referee, the 2i/c was relegated to watching the next game from the sidelines. Always one for getting stuck in, both as player and spectator, he did overstep the mark when we lost possession near the opposition's touchline and their winger started off on a spectacular solo run down the side of the pitch. Unfortunately, that was the side that our 2i/c was standing on.

As the player hurtled down the pitch we could only stand and watch as he headed for a great and certain touchdown. That was until he neared our illustrious officer. Never one to give up easily or allow the opposition to dictate the game, he stepped over the sideline and stopped the winger dead in his tracks, with a beautiful right hook to the chin.

A Dose Too Far

After a recent military exercise to East Africa one of the young soldiers in the unit had to report sick to the emergency department of the local military hospital.

The soldier asked to see a doctor as he had a rather personal problem and did not want to be seen by one of the female nurses. Finally he agreed to see a male nurse in one of the examination cubicles. Asked what the problem was, the shy and somewhat embarrassed young soldier explained that he had blood coming from the end of his penis.

As the nurse examined the penis the soldier was quizzed as to what he thought might have caused this. Had he been kicked in the groin while playing sports, been involved in a fight or some lurid sex act perhaps?

With much coaxing he finally explained that during his recent tour the older men had paid for him to lose his virginity to a local prostitute: "Take this boy and bring back a man".

Like the good soldier he was, the young lad had listened intently to the pre-deployment medical briefings and had been shocked to learn that the country was a hotbed of venereal disease. After his night of passion he had religiously checked each day for sores or any discharge. He became so obsessed with this that he resorted to using a lead pencil as a dipstick and had been inserting it into his urethra to see if there was any yellow pus. This was bad enough but he had been inserting it sharp point first and had shredded the lining of his urethra, hence the bloody discharge.

Scared? What, Me?

Compulsory fitness training is a factor of military life, no matter where you are in the world or what unit you are in. So one day I'm in a squad of about twenty soldiers being led around the countryside by one of our muscle-bound Physical Training Instructors. We had run four or five miles at a brisk pace when all of a sudden the instructor veers left, vaults over a farm gate and leads us off across a farmer's field. Not even halfway across the instructor lets out a whimpes and a few expletives, hastily about-turns the squad and, at high speed, encourages us to follow him back out of the field.

Unfortunately for this intrepid pumper of iron he was scared to death of cows and the field he had tried to traverse had two fat old dairy cows standing in the far corner.

Visiting Other Units

I was once asked to lecture a small select band of soldiers from another regiment. They were going to form a COPs[10] team when that regiment deployed to Northern Ireland. The request was a personal one and had come from their RSM who was a friend of mine.

Having collected all the equipment required for the lectures, I departed, along with a sergeant who would assist me during the training. We drove to their camp in the afternoon and were booked into the Sergeants' Mess for the two evenings we were staying. Good SNCOs that we were, one of the first things we did was to read the Mess Rules to acquaint ourselves with meal times, dress codes and bar times. We then set about checking the layout of the camp and in particular the lecture theatre we would use next morning.

Once this was all done and we were happy that all was set for an early start next morning we decided to go out of camp for a beer and return later to the Mess to meet some of the other SNCOs. We had noted that the Mess dress code for that evening was 'collar and tie, jackets optional'. So taking ties with us we headed for the camp gate. At the gate we turned left and went into the first pub we found.

Not the friendliest of places, it was obviously a squaddie bar none the less, so we had two beers and then walked back to the Sergeants' Mess. As we went in and out of the main gate, past the guardroom, we noted that the soldiers had to parade for inspection. On their way out the inspection was to ensure that they were clean and smart, on their way back in it was to prove that they were in a fit and good order. We also noted that everybody ran, at the double, when inside the barracks, either in uniform or civilian clothes.

Arriving in the Mess we went off to the cloakroom, dropped off our coats and put our ties on. Then, on entering the bar, as required by Army etiquette, we introduced ourselves and asked the barman for two beers. However, the barman stated that we could not be served. Why? we asked, and were told that we were improperly dressed. Not understanding this I went off to speak to the senior Mess member present and asked what the problem was. He informed me that the dress for the evening was in fact 'collar, tie and jackets'.

'But we checked the Mess Rules and it stated "Collar and tie, jackets optional"', I said.

'Ah! But not on every third Tuesday, when it's ladies' bingo in the Mess' says he.

Looking around I could not see any ladies at all. 'But where are they?', I inquired.

'Just because no one's turned up doesn't mean that you can come in improperly dressed', was the reply.

With that we walked straight out of the Mess and returned to the pub we had just vacated.

Next morning, and after my first two lectures, I went off to the Regimental Headquarters and, in true military fashion, paid my compliments to the RSM to say thanks for inviting us down to lecture his troops.

After the usual pleasantries, the RSM stated that we had caused quite a stir the evening before. I started to explain about the misunderstanding over the dress in the Mess, but he was on about something else. It appears that we had chosen to drink in the only local pub the Junior Ranks are allowed to go in. We should have used the one on the opposite side of the road which is exclusively for SNCOs. A pub further down the street turns out to be for officers only.

The Colonel's Bum

During the course of lectures mentioned above, one of the topics was the administration of intramuscular painkillers and antibiotics. This would be needed if anyone was injured or ill while out on COP tasks, for they would not be able to compromise the location by leaving it in an emergency nor could they get picked up quickly to be returned for proper medical assistance.

Having demonstrated the techniques required I was just about to split the students up into pairs, so that they could practise on each other, when the Commanding Officer came into the lecture theatre. Once we were introduced by the RSM, he inquired what we were doing and I explained it to him. Very impressed, he stated that he really ought to know how to do this as he might go out with the COPs team.

Singling out the youngest member of the COPs team, I announced that he would pair off with the CO and have the pleasure of injecting two millilitres of sterile water into his colonel's backside.

The colonel went first and made rather a good job of it, much to the amusement of the students and causing the odd comment that he had obviously used hypodermic needles before. The young soldier was not too sure about this at all and took some persuading that if he hurt the CO the RSM was not going to throw him in jail.

Having correctly loaded the water into the syringe and with a large bore needle attached, the young lad advanced on the colonel's exposed backside. Shaking like a leaf he forgot all the advice I had given about using a sharp dart-throwing technique to get the needle into the skin. Instead, with a very shaky hand, he slowly pushed the needle through the skin and into the muscle.

Knowing how painful that would have been, I noted the grin on everyone's face, including the RSM's, and by the grimace on the colonel's it was clear that that the young soldier had achieved some form of sadistic pleasure in sticking something up the CO's backside.

Man Overboard

Ordered to carry out joint service training with the Royal Navy, we descended on the naval base by private car. We were stopped and searched at the gate, then directed where to park and I drove round to find a space in the designated car park just across the road from our temporary billet. As I chatted to the others in our group, I unloaded my cases. I had just stepped onto the grass verge that separated the car park from the road when a loud whistle sounded followed by the order to 'stand still'. We all looked round to see a rather fierce looking Naval Shore Patrol running towards us. Standing still as ordered, I dropped my cases and waited to see what was going on.

Asked by the Petty Officer in charge of the patrol who I was, I offered my military ID card and explained my identity.

'Just stand still and wait for the life preserver to be thrown to you', he said.

'What life preserver?' I asked. 'Is this some silly joke?'

'Listen', he retorted, 'the captain of this ship, or camp as you would call it, has declared that anyone on the grass is to be classed as Man Overboard and we have to deal with them.'

So I stood there and one of the patrol threw a life preserver all of two feet to me and then pulled the safety line in as I walked off the grass. Recording my name, number and unit details, he stated that the Master at Arms would be sending a report of the incident to my unit for them to deal with.

Two nights later we had finished the training exercise, so we headed for a local hostelry for refreshments. As we arrived at the front gate and were about to pass through, a naval policeman stepped out of the guardroom and wanted to know where we were going.

'Off on the town for a few beers', we replied.

'Not tonight,' said he, 'the captain has declared No Gangway for the evening.'

'What does that mean in English?' one of us asked.

'No shore leave', he answered.

'But we are on land and we are Army personnel.'

'Ohh', says the policeman 'Well. If anyone asks, you jumped ship and swam ashore', and he walked back into the guardroom.

Officer's Batman

Deployed in Central America, I lodged in a camp occupied by a company from one of our most prestigious foot regiments. They were a funny bunch with their own rules and regulations. One of them was that senior officers still have a batman appointed to look after them.[11] In this particular company the Officer Commanding (OC) had a much prized batman.

The soldier had attended the Royal Military Academy, Sandhurst, just as his father had and his father before that. However, unlike his ancestors, he was not to become a senior officer in the family's regiment as, much to their embarrassment, he failed the commission-

25

ing course. Under the threat of disinheritance he was made to join up as an enlisted rank and had to serve a minimum of six years. He was also reputed to be the richest man in the company.

Early one morning I was sitting on the steps of my billet talking with the chap who would take over my duties in two days' time. As we chatted about the situation we noted the OC's batman running down the hill from the Officers' Mess.

You must remember that although this was a jungle location, the batman was still required to wear a white starched shirt, black bow-tie, highly polished shoes and neatly pressed uniform trousers.

We watched as he ran to the vehicle park, jumped into a Land Rover and drove quickly out of the camp. After half an hour or so we saw him drive back into the camp and run up the hill to the Officers' Mess. The poor lad was sweating heavily and looked more that a little cheesed off.

Later that day we cornered the batman and asked what all the fuss was earlier. It transpired that the OC always had a fried breakfast followed by toast and honey.[12] This particular morning, however, the officer was not amused to find the honey pot empty. As there were no replacement pots in the store the batman was ordered to dash off and buy some.

When he returned to the dining room, lathered up like a racehorse, the officer reprimanded him for having creases in his shirt and stated that he did not require the honey any more as the toast had gone cold.

Smoke Can Damage Your Health

When enjoying myself in Central America I had the pleasure of working in a small remote location with some members of the Royal Engineers.[13] Their task was to build and maintain the numerous small outposts and various camps around the country. Unsurprisingly, the REs are a 'play hard, work hard' bunch of people, who relish the simple diversions available in such situations. These being fitness training, jogging, football or rugby, fighting and drinking and upsetting lesser mortals whenever possible.

Also occupying this camp was a company of infantry, with whom the REs did not get on too well. There had been a few run-ins between the two units, both on a one-to-one basis and at unit level.

One Sunday afternoon I sat with most members of the RE troop that were based in the camp and had a few cold beers with them. The troop bar area was a palm leaf and attap construction with a circular serving area in the middle. And as it was a particularly sweltering hot day, the barman was naked and sitting in the beer cooler, while we lolled about on, or under, the homemade bench seats and tables.

As the day progressed some of the lads went off to eat or catch an hour's sleep before rejoining the party. Later that evening and through a rather drunken haze, I did notice that two of the lads had been away for some time and that when they returned, they were being very enigmatic, even secretive, about something. We found out what that was about an hour later.

After leaving the bar the two lads had gone across camp to where the infantry had set up their Junior Ranks Bar. Stealthily the two had manoeuvred around the outside of the building (it was a medium-sized affair constructed out of corrugated iron sheets on a wooden frame) and closed the hurricane shutters over the windows. This had gone unnoticed as some thirty soldiers were inside watching a movie at the time and the lights were turned down. The coup de grâce was the fact they had activated two large smoke grenades just prior to securing the only exit with a metal stake.

When the poor old infantry were finally released, they emerged coughing, spitting and eyes watering, and with sweaty skin and clothes stained a very dainty shade of orange.

Coffin Drill

One afternoon as I moved around a Guards unit I saw a squad of Junior NCOs on the Drill Square. These poor souls were attending an NCOs' Promotion Course and were brushing up on their foot drill skills. This particular session entailed practising all the drill movements used during a military funeral and, at the time, I noticed that they were carrying out Coffin Drill. This meant marching around in slow and quick time with an actual coffin on their shoulders. A Drill Instructor was barking out orders as eight of the students formed the burial party, while the remainder of the course stood at ease on the edge of the square waiting their turn in the squad.

Just as I passed the square I heard a voice, seemingly coming from heaven, calling out 'Halt that Squad Sergeant'. This was the unit RSM as he marched o to the hallowed ground of the Drill Square and approached the squad. Intrigued as to what was going on, I slipped around the corner of a building to watch this rather curious activity, made more so by the fact that just behind the RSM marched a private soldier carrying a chair. RSMs are gods in the Army and never more so than in a Guards unit.

The RSM marched towards the coffin-carrying squad, who now stood ramrod straight at attention. After a short conversation with the Drill Instructor, the RSM marched up to the side of the squad, halted correctly and pointed to the ground with his pace-stick. The private then positioned the chair on that spot as directed by the RSM.

Was he going to sit there and watch the squad in action? No, with great military precision and the regulation pause of 'two-three', he stepped on to the chair, bent at the waist, and began shouting at the top of his voice. I'm sure that I saw the peak cap on his head spin round and steam shoot out of his ears as well.

The coffin was unceremoniously dropped to the ground and a soldier, who had been lying in it to make the weight correct, was hauled out and quick-marched, under escort, to the guardroom. It appears that he was not lying to attention in the coffin and was jailed for his sloppy behaviour.

Just a Normal Working Day

One of the things I will remember from my Army service will be the hassle, time-wasting and usually totally pointless bull that goes into a senior officer's visit to your unit. I will recount only one such visit but please do not think that this was in any way an isolated case.

When I was the RSM of a certain unit we received instructions from HQ UK Land Forces, via District HQ and Garrison HQ, that we were to be blessed with a visit from a Very Very Senior General. However, great emphasis was laid to the fact that this was to be an INFORMAL VISIT DURING A NORMAL WORKING DAY.

Thus the first thing that happened, some three weeks prior to the main visitation, was that we were subjected to a very formal Garrison Commander's inspection. The Garrison Commander, who was a typical fastidious, pedantic fuddy-duddy, was destined to be retired after commanding nothing more spectacular than a Garrison HQ and a small collection of personnel best described as 'odds and sods'. He toured the unit lines and pointed out where our illustrious visitor was to be shown and where he was not to be allowed. He also picked out unit members that were to be positioned around the camp so that the General could talk to them. He insisted that certain unit activities be staged and that various stores, workshops and offices were to be instantly redecorated.

The week before the VIP was due, we had to perform a complete run-through of the programme, down to the exact timing of each phase of the intended visit. This was carried out by one of the General's senior ADCs[14] acting as the General himself. Everything had to be just as if it were the event itself and included following the precise route the visit would take, meeting all the pre-positioned staff while checking their answers to prearranged questions. Any unwanted background noise or activities had to be halted, any props or equipment to be used were checked, along with office lighting and décor. Even telephones were to be disconnected so that they would not ring while our illustrious leader was in an office.

The great day arrived and like actors on first night we all nervously awaited the great man himself. Needless to say that he arrived thirty-five minutes late, after having a prolonged luncheon in a neighbouring garrison's Officers' Mess. When he finally stepped out of his car, it was obvious that he had eaten something or perhaps drunk too much wine with his lunch, as he had become rather travel sick during the twenty-minute journey and had vomited several times in the back of his armoured staff car. Much to the annoyance of the ADC and armed civilian police bodyguard that travelled with him.

He had also become somewhat disorientated, which made some think that he was suffering from the advanced stages of Korsakoff's syndrome (typicaly alcohol-induced). One of the things he was supposed to ask each of our pre-positioned unit members was how long they had been in this particular garrison. But he continually named a totally different garrison for which he received rather blank stares. This further confused him and he would wander off muttering about how stupid the young soldiers and officers of today were.

As we meandered around the unit lines trying to keep our visitor to the agreed route and timings, I managed to ask the police bodyguard how he got on with the said man. His reply was as honest as you could get and totally straightforward. Basically he stated that the great man himself could not sack him, jail him or demote him and that at the end of the working day he could go home to his family and forget about the 'old git' until the next day.

At the end of this débâcle, which had lasted just less than the pro-grammed two hours twenty minutes, the General held a man-to-man debrief with the Commanding Officer. The outcome of which was that the General would be urgently seeking the removal of the CO. It tran-spired that the heinous crime perpetrated by the Colonel was that he had conducted the initial unit presentation in his office with three sheets of A4 paper on his desk, when it should have been totally clear of all such items.

Needless to say that when this minor peccadillo was explained to senior commanders, the Colonel was allowed to continue with his tenure in command of the unit and nothing more was said.

So much for an INFORMAL VISIT DURING A NORMAL WORKING DAY.

Trust Me, I'm an Officer

One of the highlights in any unit's calendar is the annual visit from the Officer in Charge of Manning and Records Office (OIC MRO). This is the man that ultimately authorises postings, trade changes, courses, promotions and discharges. Therefore he is a relatively important person who all liked to listen to. Nevertheless, after many years in the Army, you can just about do the presentation yourself. It rarely changes and the odd slide and viewfoil are seen time and again.

This particular year the visit was to be conducted by the new OIC MRO, who had been in post for just over six months, so we all wanted to listen to him just in case he had anything new to say. He started his presentation by emphasising that he would be making his office a more caring and compassionate establishment than in previous times.

If anyone had any problems then he would do his best to take a sympathetic stance and sort the matter out.

At the end of his still tedious and unilluminating presentation, the audience was given a few minutes to ask questions. One young NCO stood up and explained that he was due to be posted to Germany in the near future and his wife, who was also a serving NCO, was due to move to a different garrison also in Germany. His question to the OIC MRO was, Would there be any chance of them being posted to the same garrison?

The new OIC MRO's answer reaffirmed all our beliefs that nothing had really changed, when he stated, 'If you don't like how your career is planned and where you're posted to, then perhaps it's time to consider leaving the Army'.

Male v. Female

I had been asked to umpire a unit field exercise on a training area not far outside our garrison. The unit under scrutiny had a fair proportion of females and the senior ranking female was a formidable major.

The unit had deployed to the training area, via trucks and Land Rovers, this taking only forty-five minutes from their barracks. While the male members of the unit set the vast array of tentage up and carried out other manual and mundane tasks, the females were shown around the location by the female major who was in charge of their detachment. They sat talking as the men sweated and toiled; they were first in the meal queue and even managed a few hours' sunbathing after lunch. Needless to say, the male soldiers were not amused.

As night fell the all-male guard was deployed out to the perimeter; the girls sat in one of the tents chatting with soft drinks, purchased for them by the major on one of her many trips to the local shops. She had convinced the Commanding Officer to allow her, and only her, to bring her green MG sports car into the exercise area. As it was green, she contested that she could park it at the entrance to the training area and no one would really notice it.

The leisurely life of the females continued the next day as the rest of the unit prepared for a forty-eight hour NBC[15] exercise. Male

31

soldiers had to carry their webbing and weapon with them at all times; however, the females were exempt from this on orders of the major. She also contested that the females were not there to perform nasty, dirty, sweaty manual preparations but would carry out their role as administrators, clerks, cooks and other such duties once everything was set up and the exercise proper began.

Mutterings and rumours of mutiny greatly increased that evening when it was announced that the females were to be allowed back to barracks so that they could shower and change their clothes. Male officers and senior ranks protested to the CO but to no avail. The female major had insisted that it was essential for the girls to have this privilege for their health and medical wellbeing and the CO, not the strongest military leader I had encountered, had capitulated to another awful gender-based gaff.

Later that night the four-tonne truck with the girls on board re-entered the exercise area. You did not have to hear this, as you could smell the perfume, hair lacquer and non-tactical body applications for a few miles around. The major had, of course, used her MG sports car for this most necessary of female military duties.

Next morning the NBC exercise started and everyone was busy with this, except the female major, who had to nip to the shops for a newspaper. Unfortunately, she had a problem with her sports car door locks, which seemed jammed and she also noted that for some inexplicable reason the paintwork was changing colour. She summoned the second-in-command, who called the SNCO in charge of the motor pool; he managed to free the door lock but could offer no explanation for the colour change.

At the end of the exercise we returned to barracks and I joined some of the unit members for drinks in the bar. It transpired that most of the troops had noted, with some disgust, the male-female inequality demonstrated during the exercise and had expressed their abhorrence by using the female major's car as a focal point for one of their essential male functions, urination.

Married Quarters

One of my Army buddies had just got married and had been allocated married quarters in one of the old Victorian blocks that dominated our end of the garrison. These married quarters used to be cavalry barracks, with the ground floor used as stables and the first floor as the men's accommodation. My mate, a corporal, had married a QA[16] nurse, who was also a corporal and they were promised that they would not have to stay in these quarters for very long before being re-housed.

Almost nine months later he was called from the unit lines to be told by the Married Quarters Estate Warden that he had to move into a new house that day.[17] The new quarters were at the other end of the garrison so some of us volunteered to help and we managed to get the use of a military lorry as well. Even so it took us well into the evening to finish off this piece of well-thought-out family welfare. His wife was working on the wards at the local military hospital and could not get immediate time off to see her new home before she moved into it.

The next day demolition of the old Victorian blocks started and a few weeks later my friend was amazed to receive a large bill from the Estate Warden's office for redecoration of his old quarters. When he complained about this he was told that he had used an unauthorised colour scheme to decorate the now demolished married quarters and the rules were very strict about what could and could not be done in married quarters.

He had to pay the bill and then redress the action through the correct administrative channels. In total, it took him nearly two years to get his money back.

New in The Country

Having just arrived at my new unit in Germany I was asked to attend a Warrant Officers' lunch that was being held in our Sergeants' Mess, hosted by our RSM, for warrant officers in the garrison. It would be an excellent chance to meet not only the warrant officers from my own unit but also warrant officers from all the other units in the area.

The meal was splendid, as was the badinage between all those present. Afterwards we adjourned to the Mess bar and continued the banter and inter-unit repartee normal amongst peers from various cap badges and backgrounds.

At some stage I fell into conversation with a chap from the armoured cavalry regiment just across the road from us in the garrison. He had been based in Germany for all of his eighteen-year military career and could not understand that it was my first posting to the country, in fact he became quite belligerent. Through the effect of copious amounts of alcohol, he thought that I was actually lying to him.

The discussion was settled when my RSM, and his, came across and pointed out to him that some people in the forces do not have to serve their entire career in Germany and that there are other places in the world to serve. To make things worse I found out that after all the time he had spent in the country he could not speak more than a couple of words of the language.

Standby Germany

It was during my short stint in Germany, or BAOR[18] to be politically correct, that I came to believe that if the Russian Army had wanted to invade Western Europe, then the best time would have been from mid- afternoon Friday until Sunday evening on any weekend.

This piece of military strategy was formulated after seeing what happened in the average BAOR unit after dismissal on any given Friday. Normally the junior ranks headed to the NAAFI; the senior ranks went to their respective Messes and the officers just disappeared. Even so, the effect of all this movement would be the same: by one on Saturday morning everybody (except the unit guard hopefully) would be drunk and incapable.

Some units had their own all-ranks clubs, where beer would be quaffed in vast amounts by all hands until either the call from the local bars, discos, brothels, or married quarters dragged the participants away. Grievances stored up during the previous working week, sports events or social encounters would regularly erupt into fights and rank had no privilege here.

For most, the rest of the weekend would pass wrapped in the vapours of alcohol. A few would venture out in their cars to visit friends in other units, some would journey to the hotspots of Europe, such as Amsterdam or Hamburg; using up their stocks of BAOR petrol coupons.[19] However, for the majority the farthest they went was to their favourite local watering hole.

This type of behaviour was not confined to BAOR or just to the British Forces in Europe. One of our NATO allies would allow their camps to close down completely at weekends, not even to be manned by a rear party. While others would open their main gates after Friday lunch and all except the guard would stream out and head home.

One of the things that amazed me was that no record was kept for the whereabouts of unit personnel during these periods. No booking-in or out register was kept at the guardroom so, if the Russians did attack, no recall system could be initiated to defend our area of responsibility.

Him and His Stick

One of the commanding officers that I had to endure had the worst case of halitosis it was ever my misfortune to come across. He also had the annoying habit of carrying a steel-tipped Blackthorn walking stick at all times, even in civilian clothes I'm sure. In some regiments it was/is traditional for officers to carry Blackthorns but not in this one, and certainly not a Blackthorn as large as this officer used to drag around. I always imagined that he viewed this as a substitute field marshal's baton.

Before I continue, however, I must state that most COs that I served under were excellent and it was a pleasure to have known and worked for them. Nevertheless there were a few that I remember well, and these were usually complete and utter spare parts, who would have had a job sustaining a military career as a private soldier let alone as a commissioned officer.

Back to the plot. Our beloved colonel would wander around using his walking stick as a pointer or prodder of people and places, and would sometimes use it as a leaning post.

One particular day, he could think of nothing useful to gainfully employ his personnel so he ordered us to set up his Field Command Post. He wanted the full array of materiel[20] used for this little time-wasting exercise, including what was then a very new liner system that would supposedly protect the staff inside from chemical and biological warfare agents.

Once this was all set up and ready for his inspection, he was escorted out of his headquarters by the Second-in-Command, the adjutant and the RSM. The lucky ones had to wear NBC respirators and hence did not have to suffer the CO's paint-stripping bad breath, the remainder just had to hold their breath and hope that he did not ask them a question or talk directly at them. Inside the command post he busied himself with asking questions about this bit of equipment and that piece of paper, all items that he had seen a thousand times before. On entering the new liner system through an airlock, the CO was greeted by the sergeant in charge, and as they spoke the CO leant on his Blackthorn stick. In doing so he managed to puncture the flooring, rendering that liner inoperable. Slightly embarrassed by this he continued his inspection and went through into the next area. As he was about to point to a certain piece of equipment he swung the stick around ripping a large hole in the roofing fabric. Finally, deciding enough was enough, he graciously gave the order to pack everything away and take the whole thing back to the stores.

The outcome of this inspection was that thirty personnel wasted a day setting up, manning and dismantling the command post just so that the colonel could meander through it for the hundredth time since he took command. He then went back to his office and, in consultation with his quartermaster, decided how he was to justify the 'write-off' of over £4,000 of taxpayers' money caused by his walking stick.

When it came time for this CO to hand over command, the Blackthorn disappeared. On the last day of his tenure the officers gathered in the HQ for drinks with him. At the same time the enlisted troops gathered in the unit bar and it was then that the dreaded Blackthorn reappeared. To much applause it was ceremoniously snapped into small pieces before being taken to the unit carpenter's shop and reduced to wood chip. When the CO came into the bar to say his heartfelt farewell he was presented with an engraved tankard which, for safety, was packed in a box surrounded with wood chip.

Runaway Soldier

One afternoon, as I sat in my office, I received a phone call from the

36

local Royal Military Police (RMP) asking if I had an empty cell in the unit guardroom and, as the unit RSM, would I give them permission to place a soldier under arrest in my jail overnight. In fact it was a very quiet period in the unit and I had plenty of cells empty plus a provost sergeant only too eager to look after some miscreant.

The arrangements were agreed and they turned up less than an hour later with their prisoner. Once he was installed in the jail the two escorting RMPs came into my office to fill me in on the background to his offences. It transpired that the lad had just been released from the Services Psychiatric Hospital and had travelled to the home of his ex-wife. There he had trashed the place and assaulted the lady. The civil police had arrested him and handed him over to the military authorities.

Those military authorities, as it turned out, had been the local military hospital where he was to be examined by a doctor with the view to re-admitting him to the psychiatric hospital for further evaluation. While awaiting that examination the soldier had escaped from his escort and disappeared, only to be re-arrested at his ex-wife's house where he was once again smashing the place up and assaulting her.

When the RMPs took over the case they were astounded to learn how, having escaped from his escort, he had made his way from the hospital back to the house. He had, in fact, walked calmly out of the hospital into the nearby garrison and flagged down a military staff car, telling the officer inside that he had to get home as soon as possible due to his wife having had an accident. The officer ordered his driver to drop the man off at the house once the officer had got out at his destination.

That particular officer was traced and once the circumstances were explained to him he was justifiably embarrassed. The soldier was taken out of my jail the next day and conveyed under RMP escort back to the psychiatric hospital.

Three-Piece Suite For Sale (Hearsay)

One of my staff sergeants was to be promoted to Warrant Officer Class Two and this meant that his rather snobbish wife insisted on moving into a much better house. As she worked for a bank it would be easy for them to get preferential mortgage rates. The staff sergeant was an extremely well liked man and a very good SNCO, but his overbearing wife ruled the roost at home.

As the date for the move drew near, a small advertisement appeared on the unit noticeboard selling items from their home. One was a living room three-piece suite that the wife deemed unsuitable for the new house. This attracted the attention of a newly married corporal who, having failed to contact the staff sergeant at work, planned to drop round the house that evening to view the three-piece suite.

Arriving in uniform, straight from work, the corporal rang the doorbell, which was answered by the lady of the house.

'Yes', she said, looking down her nose at a mere corporal who had the gross indignity of standing outside her home.

'I work with your husband and noticed that you are advertising the sale of a three-piece suite and wonder if I can have a look at it.'

'I'm sorry but my husband isn't back from work yet. When he arrives he can show you the furniture.'

'If he's not going to be long, can I wait and see him when he gets here?' asked the corporal.

'Certainly,' she replied 'but please don't wait on the doorstep. This is not a married quarters estate and our neighbours don't like the army around here. Would you mind waiting in the garage and I'll inform my husband you're there when he arrives.'

Needless to say the corporal did not bother with the three-piece suite.

Wives' Club Scandal

Most units in the Army have a Wives' Club tagged on. These can be useful social, welfare and advisory organisations. More often than not run by the CO's wife and ably assisted by the RSM's other half, they hold formal ladies' dinners and regularly have informal gatherings such as coffee mornings, Tupperware and Anne Summers parties. They do have a very useful role when the unit is deployed overseas for long periods and the families have to stay back at base.

Sometimes, however, the system goes a little haywire and backfires on its members. In this case it concerned three prominent ladies who thought they knew all that there was to know about each other.

One morning the CO's wife had cause to call on the RSM's wife to chat about the flower arrangements in the unit chapel. Knowing the RSM left for work at 7.30 each morning the CO's wife arrived at nine o'clock; not too early but possibly just in time for coffee. Knocking on the door did not get an immediate reaction but she persevered and finally the RSM's wife's head popped out of an upstairs window.

Explaining why she had come and that it would only take a few minutes, the CO's wife was allowed into the Married Quarters but considered it really bad form as the RSM's wife was still in her dressing gown at this time of day. She was invited to take a seat in the lounge while the RSM's wife went into the kitchen to put the kettle on. Once they were both equipped with a mug of coffee and the ubiquitous plate of digestive biscuits had materialised, they sat down to start chatting about Wives' Club matters. Only to be interrupted by the sound of someone moving around upstairs.

Now, the CO's wife knew only too well that there were no children in the household, something to do with medical problems or so she had heard. As the sound of feet descended to the bottom of the stairs, the RSM's wife looked decidedly uncomfortable and before she could get to the lounge door, in walked the wife of one of the unit's JNCOs, who was also an active member of the Wives' Club. Much to the embarrassment of the CO's good lady, this woman was dressed in nothing more than what was obviously the RSM's dressing gown.

Wives' Clubs being Wives' Clubs it wasn't long before the whole unit knew the sordid details. It transpired that the RSM's wife was having a liaison with the JNCO's wife and that the RSM knew all about it. It also came out that he was having a fling with another NCO's wife. The gossip got so bad that something had to be done and it all came to a head when the RSM moved his wife out of the Married Quarters, packing her off to her mother's, and moved the other lady in his life in instead. He was given a disciplinary posting out of the unit, which was in fact a three-year unaccompanied tour in the Far East, from where he finished his military service and retired.

Custard Pie, Sir?

At one stage in my life I developed a craving for custard and this coincided with a period when I was a living-in member of a certain

Sergeants' Mess.

Whenever I was dining in the Mess I would normally eat a three-course evening meal and the last dish was always a plate of custard or a custard pie. On this particular day, however, I had been invited out to a dinner party so I intended to only have a small dinner (soup and salad actually) and save myself for later.

Having finished the salad I was just about to get up from my seat, when one of the newly employed Mess stewardesses appeared with my usual dessert. For some unknown reason she got very emotional and became totally unhinged when I told her that I did not want the pie. After bursting into tears, she unceremoniously thrust the dish on to my head before running back into the kitchen howling some ear-piercing diatribe about unrequited love.

The next day I approached the Mess manager about the incident and he informed me of two factors. First, that it was compulsory, at that time, in the UK for a certain percentage of the civilian staff to be disadvantaged people, either mentally or physically challenged. Mind you, I always thought that that was why we had the Officer Cadre!

Secondly, and not surprisingly, it turned out that this woman was one of these disadvantaged employees on the Mess staff and that, since she had started working in the Mess, she had taken a motherly 'shine' to me. She would not allow any of the Mess catering staff to cook my custard treat but insisted on making the thing herself. After the incident I never saw her again, as she was re-allocated to the Officers' Mess.

Drugs Bust

One evening while I was sitting in the bar of my Sergeants' Mess, I was contacted by the RSM of the garrison's SIB[21] detachment, who wanted to know if I had any vacant cells in my guardroom. As the RSM of the unit I knew that we had, in fact, nobody at all residing in the cells. With this answer the SIB RSM asked to meet me outside the guardroom before he installed his prisoners, as there was a somewhat sensitive nature involved.

Ten minutes later I was on the veranda of the guardroom as the Royal Military Police wagon pulled up and the SIB RSM stepped out accompanied by the garrison's Provost Marshal.[22] They explained that they had four people that required overnight accommodation in single cells, prior to being seen by their commanding officer the next morning. At this stage, and very unusually, they insisted that no paperwork or records be made of the situation and the guardroom staff were to be briefed by them to ensure that they were not to talk about the matter in hand.

The plot thickened when the Provost Marshal informed me that the people involved were in fact all junior officers from the same infantry regiment in the garrison and that they had been apprehended after a drugs raid on the regiment's Officers' Mess. It transpired that several of the regiment's junior officers had converted the Mess attic into a drugs den, equipped with drinks cabinet, easy chairs and other furniture, and they would adjourn there in the evenings to partake in some 'tropical herbs', namely locally purchased cannabis.

The next day the four officers were removed under RMP escort and the next time I heard anything about them was when their courts martial were convened. This resulted in the dishonourable discharge of the four. A similar crime committed by an enlisted soldier would have resulted in a prison sentence and then a dishonourable discharge, not to mention loss of rank and/or pension rights if applicable.

Staff College Demo

Each year units from all across the sector of military life were chosen to set up a Staff College demonstration.[23] My unit was tasked to set up a training area just outside Aldershot. This meant weeks of preparation, working and full dress rehearsals, making sure that tent pegs were in line and everything was just so for the one-day visit. Equipment would be painted or shined and set out so that the visitors could see it but not touch it. Each stand or display had a viewing area separated from the actual display by white plastic tape. At most a few soldiers would act out a short scenario as an SNCO or officer explained the display.

At one of our stands, a very timorous staff sergeant had to deliver a lengthy speech about the unit's planned movements across a flat featureless plain in central Germany, as if we were advancing against our once arch enemy, the Russians. No matter how many times this SNCO practised he could not remember it parrot fashion. Hand-held scripts we were told were an absolute no-no and no variation was allowed from the prepared text either.[24] After several days of rehearsals I attended yet another run-through and was amazed that the staff sergeant was obviously reading the words from cue cards hidden around the display. He should never have been chosen for this role; since being nominated he had developed a nervous twitch and a pronounced stammer. None the less the powers that be within the unit would not replace him, coming out with old clichés like 'it will be character building' and 'he'll have to learn to project himself if he wants to get on in the Army'. (As he was a staff sergeant with twenty years' service I thought he had already progressed within the Army.)

Having been told that his presentation was too stilted and still not up to standard, he had to think up another way of hiding his script. The next day we had the final dress rehearsal with some senior officers playing the part of the visitors. When they arrived at the staff sergeant's stand he was horrified to see that they stood right up front against the white tape barrier, causing it to stretch and twist.

Starting his address rather well he suddenly began to falter, stuttering and going completely off at a tangent to his script. Fortunately this group of officers did not know the correct text and went off to the next stand muttering threats of disembodiment if he did not get it right for the big show. When they departed we returned to the staff sergeant to find out what had gone wrong this time. So he could look straight at the audience and recite his piece, he had written some of the key words along his side of the tape barrier. Unable to read it he had jumped ahead and continued from his cue cards. Nevertheless, drastic action was needed, as the demonstration proper was due in two hours. The poor SNCO was at his wits' end and close to a nervous breakdown.

Later, during the actual demonstration, the staff sergeant delivered an impeccable oration, as the unit had finally reneged and provided him with a lectern so that he could read the script verbatim from his notes. Not one of the visitors or Staff College faculty commented on this and the whole demonstration was deemed an unmitigated success.

Climb Every Mountain

One year I was asked to participate in a military expedition to climb the highest mountain in North Africa-Mount Toubkal in Morocco. After many months of planning, we departed on an RAF flight to Gibraltar where we were to stay for twenty-one days, supposedly carrying out final training and preparation. We had the run of the beach, the RAF Sergeants' Mess, and of course the nightlife. Two civilianised Land Rovers and trailers were loaded up with all our kit and we finally headed across the Straits of Gibraltar by ferry to Tangier.

Taking a leisurely route to the High Atlas Mountains, via Rabat, Fez, Casablanca and Marrakech, we struck out for Mount Toubkal. The ascent took us two days, during which civilian holidaymakers in summer clothes and sandals surrounded us. Halfway up the mountain is a collection of small huts with a kiosk selling refreshments. At the summit a collage of photographs was taken as evidence that we had reached the top and our descent was completed in a day. It was then back through Marrakech to Tangier and the ferry across to Gibraltar. Total time in Morocco was seven days.

Once back on the Rock, we were allowed to spend another seven days de-acclimatising and getting over any effects from our time at high altitude. A nice comfortable RAF VC10 flight back to the UK completed this arduous and testing expedition.

Non-Driver Wants Assistance

One fine year I was ordered to Germany for a month's detachment. A fellow staff sergeant, who manned a small outpost, needed to get an ordinary driving licence and I was to stand in for him while he took the lessons and test. Evidently he had waited months for this opportunity and required the licence to enhance his career. Why he hadn't done this before and why he was posted into that appointment without a licence, when one was needed to do the job, was beyond me. However, orders were orders, so off I trundled.

After three weeks in post I learnt that the staff sergeant was due to take his test the following Monday and once successful I could return to my parent unit back in the UK. But, as with most things in life, nothing went according to plan.

The night before the test the staff sergeant went off for a few beers in a local tavern. Leaving in the early hours he was stopped by the German civil police and charged with being drunk in charge of a bicycle. Not only did he incur the wrath of the military authorities,[25] but he had his driving licence suspended for one year from whenever he finally passed his test.

Wanted: One Chef

In one unit the master chef, a staff sergeant from the Army Catering Corps, had developed a real dislike for one of his lance corporal chefs, to the extent of trying to frame him on a charge of theft.[26] One evening when that particular chef was on late duties in the unit cookhouse, the master chef briefed the guard commander that he suspected that the young chef would try to steal food at the end of his duty and take the contraband to his married quarters. I was, and still am, convinced that some form of pressure was exerted on the guard commander by the master chef, as a semi-covert operation was mounted to observe the back of the cookhouse and storerooms at the time the chef finished his duty.[27]

At the end of his shift the young chef correctly secured the cookhouse, rations stores and refuse areas. Then, before leaving the unit lines he handed the keys in to the guardroom, in fact he handed the keys to the guard commander, who logged the event in the guardroom Occurrence Book.

Nevertheless, the next morning the lance corporal was called in front of the RSM and accused of stealing food the previous evening. Two of the guards provided written and verbal statements to the effect that, on the orders of the guard commander, they had maintained observation on the chef as he left and that they had seen him loading foodstuff into the boot of his car. The master chef, who, having carried out a quick stock-check, stated that two large cartons of vegetables, a carton of baked beans and a side of pork were all missing from the cookhouse.

Having listened to the evidence against him the NCO asked to speak in his own defence.

'Sir, I may not be the brightest of soldiers or even the greatest chef ever to serve in the Army but I am not completely stupid either'.

'What do you mean by that?' asked the RSM.

'Sir, you have just been told that I was seen by two of the guards at the back of the kitchens last night loading food into the boot compartment of my car. This was immediately relayed to the guard commander back in the guardroom by radio and that he accurately recorded all the facts, as reported, in the Unit Occurrence Book. There are two problems there as I see them, sir.'

'What are they then?' quizzed the RSM.

'First, sir. If they had already seen me take the food why did they let me leave camp with it? Secondly, sir, and more importantly, they state that I loaded the food into boot of my car. Sir, I have a VW Beetle!'[28]

The accusations against the JNCO were dropped. The two guard members concerned were interviewed by the RSM and Unit Adjutant, in some depth, but no action was taken against them. The Master Chef and Guard Commander were posted out of the unit.

Map Reading

While attending a senior promotion course we were required to learn the finer points of map reading and navigation. Unfortunately, the instructor for this phase of the training was not a natural teacher; in fact he was to teaching what Leonardo da Vinci was to arc welding. To make matters worse he insulted all our intelligences by starting the lectures with a large blank sheet of white paper on which he drew a series of lines to explain about grid squares on a map.

During a later lecture he began to lose the thread of things when we bombarded him with questions about 'back-bearings' and 'intervisibility'. Finally, when we asked about astronavigation, the use of sun compasses and global positioning systems, he threw his arms in the air and stormed out of the classroom. From that period on we spent the rest of our map-reading classes out on the local training area doing orienteering competitions.

I do not wish to undermine the validity of promotion courses but during a similar course we had to learn about communications procedures. The instructor for this topic also ran the unit boxing team and much preferred to be with them than us. To facilitate this, at the start of the first lecture he presented us with the communications test paper that would form part of the final course examination. Thereafter he would pop in at the beginning of each lesson, check that all was well, and disappear with his beloved boxing team.

Needless to say we all scored highly in our communications examination and praise was heaped upon the instructor for his training skills.

Tent Pegs

Each year the Regular Army Assistance Tables (RAATs) would be published and these laid down what each unit, formation and district must do to assist other units.[29] One year we had to provide tentage and personnel for a military reunion at a national park in the south of England. As the theme for the weekend was 'Past and Present', we had to supply old-style marquees, vintage vehicles and equipment. We were required to have personnel dressed in First World War uniforms.

After months of planning and raiding museums up and down the country for equipment and clothing, we deployed the entire unit to the national park for two whole weeks. This commitment meant that we would be at full stretch and could only afford to leave a small rear party behind to guard the camp and one clerk to man the Orderly Room.

Our temporary base was set up just outside the park in the grounds of an old police college, which was only a few hundred yards from our intended display site. Here the RSM and myself, as the Senior Warrant Officer Class Two, set our own tent up and, being slightly eccentric, we used orange plastic tape to mark out a small rectangle of grass adjacent to the tent door; this was then signposted as the Warrant Officers' Mess. We set out a few chairs and a couple of tables so that we could relax in the Mess whenever it suited us.

The official responsibility for this RAAT tasking had been devolved to one of our officers, a captain. He was an ex-ranker who had served in such places as Tripoli (Libya) and had worked his way up through the ranks to RSM before taking his commission. He was, unfortunately, known to be a touch volatile and prone to fly off the handle at the least important thing. This was demonstrated to one and all when, on day three of our deployment, he completely lost it and damn near caused a mutiny.

On this fateful day the RSM and myself were sitting in our al fresco Mess, indulging ourselves in a bottle of fine port, when we heard screaming and shouting coming from the demonstration area. This was not just someone getting a normal bollocking but a very able attempt at verbally ripping someone to shreds. Somewhat bemused, we set out to investigate. When we arrived at the area all the soldiers were standing around as the captain in charge ranted on at one of the staff sergeants. Not wishing to interfere we waited to one side until the officer stormed off, then we called over the staff sergeant concerned and asked what had caused the outburst. He told us that the captain had gone completely mad and was stating that all the tent pegs were in the wrong way round.

Both the RSM and myself went around the site and could see nothing obviously wrong with the way the tent pegs had been set up, so we wandered off to confront the officer. The RSM was concerned as to why the officer had rebuked a SNCO in front of his men, something which goes against good military etiquette, and also as to what the officer thought was wrong with the tent pegs.

The captain had obviously got his hackles up about something and told us in no uncertain terms that, as the officer in charge of the display, he was responsible for the whole thing and if he wanted the tent pegs turned round then the tent pegs would be turned round. Not willing to listen to our point of view, we left to inform the staff sergeant to turn all the pegs round so that they conformed with the wishes of the officer.

The actual display and reunion went well, except that throughout the weekend we were inundated with questions from those old boys attending the do, as to why the tent pegs were incorrectly installed. This infuriated the RSM who, on his return to camp, photocopied pages from the Manual of Military Tentage and had them delivered to the captain's desk.

Cool Customers

Late one evening a British Army four-tonne lorry arrived at our barracks' main gate. On board were three people all in army uniform and they were in a jovial mood as they chatted to the gate guards. The visitors stated that they were transiting the area and just wanted to nip into the NAAFI to buy drinks, cigarettes and some snack food. The NAAFI was actually closed at this time of night but it was explained that there were numerous automated machines dispensing a variety of goodies, so the lorry was waved through and told that it could park adjacent to the NAAFI building. Approximately thirty minutes later the lorry exited the barracks through the main gate and disappeared off into the night.

Next morning when the NAAFI staff came in to open up the shop, canteen and leisure facilities, they were horrified to find that two of the gaming machines were missing. The fact was reported to the local police, Military Police and the unit headquarters, who all carried out thorough investigations into the theft but no one managed to identify the visiting four-tonne truck or its passengers.

The two soldiers on duty when the truck arrived and departed were castigated and spent seven days in the unit jail for failing to check identity cards and for not recording the vehicle details. The NAAFI had to replace the two machines and cover the cost of the monies lost. It was reported that there could have been upwards of £3,000 in the machines.

Air Tickets

Back in Central America I had the pleasure to work with a colonel who was rather parsimonious with his money. A fine example of this was how he misused the small hatchback car he was provided with as his service runabout. As only he and his wife used the vehicle, he removed the back seat and sold it at a local market.

He played his best trick the day he asked me to pop into a travel agency in town and buy a return air ticket for his daughter, who was a student in the UK. He wrote down her name, the flight dates and the airline he wanted her to fly on. Just before I went off I read the details again and was amazed to see that he had asked for an open-dated departure from Belize and a specified return date from the UK. Knowing that she was in the UK and travelling UK-Belize-UK, I went back and asked for confirmation.

With a completely straight face the colonel explained the rationale behind his request and that he had used this routine on several occasions without any problems. It was far cheaper to buy a return flight in Belize than it was in the UK. Hence his daughter would be sent the ticket; she would then rip out the first page, i.e. the open departure from Belize to the UK, and travel from the UK as if it were her return journey. Once in Belize she would book her UK flight using the open-dated ticket and, if anyone asked, she would explain that it had been torn out by mistake.

Want a Brew, Sir?

As RSM one of my daily tasks was to visit the unit guardroom. This allowed me to inspect the building and the guard members, to visit any prisoners we held and, more importantly, to get out of the office for an hour.

As I entered the guardroom the Provost Sergeant met me and talked me through the current guard, any problems he had and who was sitting in the cells. On one such visit, as we were about to start our tour, one of the guards asked if I wanted a brew of tea. Having accepted his offer I continued my inspection and had just started to speak to one of the prisoners when I noticed a rather pungent smell drifting into the cell. On leaving the prisoner I headed off to find the source of the smell and was amazed to find the young soldier who had offered me a cup of tea standing next to the gas stove and looking rather worried.

In his haste to gain favour with his RSM by making me a tea, he had filled the kettle and placed it on the gas burner. Unfortunately he had failed to notice that it was an electric kettle.

Nearly Caught in the Act

Regrettably some of the rules and regulations that govern the modern

Army are totally archaic and inappropriate. They can also inflict draconian punishments on the offenders. For example, the rules that governed the entertainment of the opposite sex in single servicemen's, or servicewomen's, accommodation. Generally, females were not allowed in male accommodation but males could go into female accommodation, as long as they did not go into the sleeping areas.

On entering my office one day I was informed that one of my lads had been arrested by the Military Police for being in an Out of Bounds Area, i.e. in the bedroom of a servicewoman. As the RSM I had to investigate the offence on behalf of the CO and it turned out that the lady in question was in fact the man's longstanding girlfriend. The Military Police had been called to the female accommodation block after a fellow servicewoman had noted a male entering the bedroom and reported it. When the police burst into the room they found the couple sitting drinking tea, fully clothed and watching a video.

After the male offender had been charged and found guilty by his company commander, he was remanded for CO's Orders. Prior to this I spoke to the RSM of the female offenders' unit and we agreed that the punishment should be the same for both. So when they were marched in front of their respective colonels they were both awarded fourteen days' confinement.[30]

As previously agreed with my fellow RSM, we arranged for our Soldiers Under Sentence (SUSs) to be detained in the same guardroom and they were treated to adjacent (but not connecting) cells.

Guilty by Association or Was it Assumption?

After a very pleasant but illegally extended evening in the garrison Sergeants' Mess bar, the seven of us left and headed home. We were all of warrant officer status, except for one newly promoted sergeant (he had received his promotion to acting sergeant that day), and it was his actions that led to a nasty incident in the Mess car park which had long and lasting consequences for one of us.

Throughout the evening the banter and bandying had been towards the sergeant, mainly due to the fact that he was the only one of his cap badge in the Mess.[31] Unfortunately, and perhaps due to an excess of alcohol, we had not really noticed that the young man was not taking the comments too well.

As we split up to go our separate ways, the sergeant confronted one of the group and, without explanation, head-butted the man across the bridge of his nose and then with a fierce right hook knocked out two of his front teeth. We rapidly sobered up and held the two apart, while trying to calm the situation down. However, the damage had been done: one newly promoted sergeant had struck a senior warrant officer.

Fortunately for the sergeant, the warrant officer he had assaulted did not want to pursue the issue by making an official complaint against him. It was understood that the issue had been a two-sided affair and, considering the ranks of all those present, along with the fact of illegal drinking hours, it was agreed that the matter was finished with and there was nothing further to be said. Nevertheless, the warrant officer had to report for work the next day looking as though he had fought Muhammad Ali and lost. Needless to say his commanding officer demanded an explanation and it was then that the real trouble started. The warrant officer refused to name his assailant.

After several interviews with his CO, 2i/c, and unit adjutant, the warrant officer was informed that he had to attend an interview with the RSM of the Military Police Special Investigation Branch. There he was repeatedly informed that it would be in his best interest and for the sake of proper military discipline that he name the other person. Still refusing to do so, the warrant officer was told to report back to his CO.

Once the sergeant concerned heard about the problems the warrant officer was having, he offered to step forward and accept the consequences of any disciplinary action. This, the warrant officer explained, was not necessary and would only be a foolhardy gesture from which neither would benefit.

The commanding officer ordered the warrant officer to take a few days off to fully recover and to visit the dentist, while he decided on what action would be taken and it is here that the guilt by association or assumption starts to interfere with the correct outcome.

Six years prior to this event the warrant officer was a bachelor soldier holding the rank of staff sergeant and, having drunk a vast amount of beer in the Sergeants' Mess bar one Saturday,[32] he had staggered into what he thought was his bedroom.[33] Being totally inebriated, he had failed to notice that the rightful owner of the room was actually occupying the bed onto which he had collapsed. He was found several hours later comatose, lying on the bed with the other SNCO still naked under the bed clothes. Instant accusations of homosexual practices meant the that staff sergeant was posted out of the unit and had to wait nine months before being called before a General Court Martial charged with 'commiting an act of gross indecency with another person, a male.'[34] After three days of evidence, the judge advocate advised the president and members of the court martial board that there was no actual case to answer, the staff sergeant was found not guilty and released from arrest.

Two months later he was promoted to Acting Warrant Officer Class Two and four years after being wrongfully accused he was promoted to Substantive Warrant Officer Class One. Nevertheless, the salacious and damning innuendoes would hound him for the remainder of his career.

These factors certainly affected his current commanding officer's decision who, fearing that a similar incident had occurred, resulting in an actual physical assualt on one of his warrant officers, arranged for him to be posted, at short notice, out of the unit. This did slightly backfire, as the only posting available was to a major formation which meant that the warrant officer's wages increased and he was also entitled to free of charge, fully furnished, three-bedroom married quarters.

No Laughing Please

Having just taken up his new post, the new commanding officer was found to be a very likeable leader, very much a soldier's soldier. He had originally been commissioned in the Royal Marines and it was rumoured that he had served with their special forces, the Special Boat Squadron. He actually wore a medal for service in Vietnam.

After leaving the Marines he had taken up such jobs as debt collector and reclaiming cars on which the hire purchase agreement had been defaulted. However, there was not a great deal of income from these and, having a young family at boarding school for which there was now no assistance coming in from the MoD for their fees, he had enlisted into the Army with the rank of major. After only a couple of years he had been promoted to lieutenant colonel and appointed a commanding officer.

As was the fad of the day, officers dragged a dog around with them while at work. Depending upon the officer the dog's breed would range from French poodle to African Ridge Back or from German Shepherd to Irish Wolfhound. This particular officer had a small black terrier puppy, not much bigger than a ferret and slightly over-active.

As a Warrant Officer Class Two (Company Sergeant Major) it was my job one day to parade personnel before the new CO for their arrival or departure interviews and on disciplinary orders. It was during one set of arrival interviews, when I had three new unit personnel standing to attention in front of the CO's desk, that all hell broke loose and the three soldiers collapsed in fits of laughter.

Unbeknown to me, or anyone else in the room, the CO had been sitting forward on his chair with his little dog behind him. As he had explained the virtues of a good and friendly life within his unit and what would happen if anyone transgressed his ideas of sound military bearing, the little black terrier had climbed up the back of the seat and poked its head over the colonel's shoulder.

Some Will Always Get it Wrong

One morning as I settled into my office, the guard commander (usually a corporal) from the previous night knocked on my door. It was his duty to inform me, as the unit RSM, of any unusual occurrences during his period of duty. The story he painted did not really bear thinking about but it was confirmed a few minutes later when the orderly sergeant from the same period arrived at my office door with his report.

A private soldier on duty in the unit guardroom the previous evening had been ordered, by the guard commander, to stay in the guardroom when the orderly sergeant had requested the guard commander's presence on a patrol around the unit's perimeter fence. All the other members of the guard were either manning the main gate or out on foot patrols. For some inexplicable reason, and perhaps I was being slack, we did not have any soldiers under detention in the jail that night either.

Sitting in the guardroom alone the private had decided that he was feeling cold and wanted to put on his issue heavy wool jumper. He already had his combat jacket but he wanted his jumper, so he climbed into the duty vehicle, a long wheelbase Land Rover, and nipped off to his accommodation block to fetch it. Unfortunately for him, on his way back to the now vacant guardroom, he lost control of the vehicle and crashed into a tree.

After following all due military procedures, I had to march the miscreant in front of the commanding officer so that he could be found officially guilty of the crimes he had committed, i.e. disobeying a direct order when told to stay in the guardroom, driving a military vehicle without his name on the Vehicle Work Sheet,[35] causing damage to Government property,[36] and conduct to the prejudice of good order and military discipline.[37]

As I stood behind the accused, who had been marched in front of the CO's desk, I noticed that he started to shake and tremble. On moving around to his left, I saw that he was standing to attention, upright and rigid, and crying. Just then, the CO looked up from the paperwork for the first time and saw the tears in the young lad's eyes.

'Get this man out of my office RSM', shouted the CO.

'Orders and Escort. Left turn', screamed I. 'By the front quick march'.[38]

I had just got the accused and escort out into the corridor, when the CO shouts 'RSM, tell the accused that I found him guilty and that he is sentenced to fourteen days in the jail.'

Once I had handed the accused over, who was now a 'Soldier Under Sentence' (SUS) I went back into the CO's office to collect the paperwork and charge sheet.[39] Prior to this disciplinary hearing, or 'Orders' as they are called, as was the custom, the CO and I had discussed the case and agreed on the outcome; should he be found guilty of course. We had agreed that he would get seven days in the unit jail so I wondered why the CO had changed this and sentenced him to fourteen days. He explained that he gave the soldier the additional seven days because he was a wimp and because he had cried. The CO thought that the extra would help make the lad a better man and soldier.

A Jump Too Far

Medical wellbeing is a vital part of military service. Therefore soldiers like to know that the medical staff allocated to their care are quality professionals. This, unfortunately, is not always the case.

One Regimental Medical Officer (RMO) became notorious after examining a large, very fit Fijian who had enlisted into the British Army. The soldier complained of back strain that limited his work and reduced participation in his favourite sport-rugby.

The doctor in question took a full history and then told the patient to strip completely naked (more than one of his patients had expressed their reservations about his practice of insisting that you strip naked for each examination). Once the patient was naked the RMO wandered around prodding the soldier here and there, asking the man to lean this way and that, finally coming to a diagnosis that he had a trapped nerve in his lower back.

The RMO then instructed the soldier to lie face down on the carpet so that he could free the trapped nerve. Moments later the medical centre staff were alarmed to hear a loud scream come from the Doctor's office and the medical SNCO rushed in to see what the problem was.

He was confronted by a totally naked Fijian soldier holding the much smaller RMO pinned against the office wall, feet off the ground, and just about to rearrange the RMO's facial features.

Once things had calmed down the medical SNCO ascertained that once the soldier was lying on the carpet the RMO had climbed on to his desk and jumped on to the soldiers back in an attempt to realign his lumbar vertebrae.

Another member of the medical profession to hold the post of a Regimental Medical Officer also very nearly came to a sticky end.

This particular RMO had several rather unusual propensities. One was his habit, when referring patients to hospital, to write the referral letter in various coloured inks. He might start the missive in red then change to green, before concluding in blue and signing it in orange ink. To allow him to achieve this his desk was always littered with a plethora of expensive fountain pens and bottles of ink.

His other and most annoying habit would be to arrive late for surgery and then with a waiting room full of the sick, lame and lazy, spend half an hour practising on his trumpet. To make things worse he was tone deaf and could not put two notes together to make a tune.

One day a senior warrant officer had been waiting to see the RMO for over an hour and was not best pleased when the doctor and his trumpet further delayed him. He barged into the examination room and in no uncertain terms explained to the RMO what would happen to the trumpet and his anus if he did not stop immediately or if this ever happened again.

Needless to say, once the commanding officer had been informed of the RMO's rather unmilitary behaviour, the doctor's three-year tour of duty was cut short at the six-month point and he disappeared to some far-flung corner of the British Empire.

Boxing Clever

Having the ability to drop in on your doctor any-time of the day is a great perk in the services. But it can be misused and abused. I remember a very novel way employed to stop this.

One commanding officer had decided that too many of his single or unaccompanied married chaps were sneaking off to the RMO each morning, so he instructed the adjutant to issue orders to curtail this nasty practice. The resulting directive stated that before attending sick parade potential patients must first inform their section commander, who, if he considered the medical problem severe enough to warrant seeing the RMO, would sign an authorisation for the temporary issue of MFO boxes.[40] The sick man would then have to parade at the Quartermasters' stores and be issued with the appropriate number of boxes. After dragging these back to his billet the soldier would have to pack away all his personal and military possessions into the boxes, clear his bedding back to the stores, and then hand the MFO boxes, now full, in for safekeeping.

Once this was done the soldier could attend the medical centre with his ailments or injuries, usually to find that he was in a queue behind the accompanied married men who did not have to store away the contents of their married quarters.

Present and Correct

Attending morning sick parade could be a nightmare in some regiments. After seeking permission from your company, squadron or battery office, you were expected to parade at the unit medical centre with an overnight bag just in case you were sent off to hospital or admitted the local MRS.[41] In some units you would have to be in No. 2 Dress or Parade Dress Uniform. The contents of the overnight bag would be laid down in unit standing orders.

Entering the reception or waiting area could be worse than Trooping the Colour on Horse Guards Parade. You would be expected to march up to the desk and halt in correct military fashion, or as correct as your sickness would allow. At some medical centres I visited, this would mean that you halted the correct distance from the reception desk with your feet exactly covering a set of painted boot marks on the floor. Failure to get that right would incur the wrath of the reception staff and you would be sent outside to try it again.

Once accepted into the facility you would be expected to hand over the correct paperwork as issued by your company office. A minor interrogation would then take place as to why you had deemed it necessary to report sick and on occasions the contents of the overnight bag would be inspected. Disciplinary action was promised should you not have the stated number of pairs of socks or spare laces for your boots. If all was correct you would be told to sit down in the waiting area and be called forward to see the RMO. This may be done by rank, i.e. the senior rank attending sick parade would be seen first, even if he had just walked in and you had been there for an hour.

Writing this reminds me of a much used military adage about where to find sympathy. Evidently it is in the dictionary between 'shit' and 'syphilis'.

That Thing Called an RSM

Apart from being a very powerful person in any military organisation, many RSMs have left their mark as great characters and personalities. I remember one fearsome RSM who became something of a living legend.

When starting a parade he marched onto the square, halted on his mark in front of the assembled masses, then screamed out for the Provost Sergeant to march onto the parade square and report to him.[42] Once the Provost Sergeant had halted in front of him the RSM asked him what time the parade was supposed to start.

'0945 hours, sir', replied the sergeant.

'What time is it now?' asked the RSM.

Breaking stance, the Provost Sergeant consulted his watch. '0950 hours, sir.'

'Then I'm late and the parade hasn't started on time', continued the RSM.

'Well, yes sir, I suppose that's right,' said the sergeant cautiously.

'Well sergeant, what do we do with anyone that's late on parade then?'

'We jail them, sir', acknowledged the sergeant.

'Then you had better jail me , sergeant', said the RSM and they both marched off the square and into the unit guardroom, leaving the whole parade standing to attention on the square.

On another occasion an RSM was escorting an inspecting officer through the ranks when his pace stick fell from under his left arm.[43] Halting in the correct military fashion, he retrieved it and continued with the parade. As soon as the parade was dismissed the RSM jailed his pace stick for 'conduct to the prejudice of good order and military discipline'. It stayed in the unit jail for seven days.

The best one, however, had to be when my RSM gave his wife sufficient grounds for divorce. This happened due to the fact that on certain days the unit parade square was utilised as a car park when not required for parades or other such military functions.

Looking out of his office window one day, the RSM spotted a car parked on the square. Today was one of those days that the square was needed for a parade and should not have been used for parking.

Telephoning the Provost Sergeant the RSM directed that the owner of the car should be found as soon as possible and held in the jail until the RSM has spoken to them. Yes!! It turned out to be his wife and she was held for nearly an hour before she finally convinced the Provost Sergeant to allow her to telephone the RSM's Office.

A Garrison Sergeant Major

Although Warrant Officer Class One is the most senior rank attainable as a Non-Commissioned Officer in the British Army, there are various appointments within that rank. To some rather ill-informed military personnel and most non-military types, the appointment of Academy Sergeant Major at the Royal Military Academy, Sandhurst, is believed to be the most senior appointment for soldiers. How wrong they are.

Tucked away in the Queen's Regulations for the Army is a list stating the seniority of Warrant Officer appointments and Academy Sergeant Major is not at the top of that list. In fact it is the honourable appointment of 'Conductor' that is the most senior in the Army, with Academy Sergeant Major ranking just below Garrison Sergeant Major-London District.

Now, Garrison Sergeant Major (GSM) is a funny old position and one that I never really understood.[44] Every unit has its own senior rank, whether that be Regimental Sergeant Major, Artificer Sergeant Major, or even Regimental Corporal Major.[45] So why then the need for a Garrison Sergeant Major; could they not have an RSM in charge of a Garrison HQ unit?

I have in fact met some very odd GSM situations. At one Garrison Sergeants' Mess I stayed in, the GSM was the President of the Mess as it was deemed to be his Mess. However, the two Conductors that lived in the Mess could outrank him. At another Garrison Mess, the GSM would never come into the Mess bar as he was a reformed alcoholic and thought all drinkers were something close to Satan. He would insist on drinking fruit juices when attending a formal function or regimental dinner and was even known to put lemonade into an empty beer can so that it looked as though he was joining in the action and being one of the boys at an informal event.

On one occasion when the Mess was graced with the presence of royalty, the GSM met their Royal Highnesses as the car arrived, escorted them into the Mess and introduced them to the Mess staff. He then handed them over to the next most senior Mess member, who escorted them into the bar area where he introduced the military members present to their Royal Highnesses. When the visit finished the GSM met the royal party in the corridor outside the bar area and escorted them back to their car.

Trouble for Two

Having spent a pleasant evening at my local pub I returned to the Sergeants' Mess for a nightcap. It was permissible to join the bar as long as you arrived before 2300 hours and were not too drunk and considered properly dressed. On entering the bar, and in keeping with correct Mess etiquette, I asked the senior member present for permission to have a drink. On this occasion it was the RQMS[46] and he invited me to join him and the two other Mess members at the bar, in fact they were the only three members in the bar at the time. However, there were two ladies sitting at the other end of the bar who I thought were guests of those I had joined.

About forty-five minutes later the barman, a serving corporal in the unit, came to us and asked if there were any last orders as he was going to close the bar.

'What do you mean-close the bar?' gasped the RQMS. 'I'm the senior member present and I say when the bar closes. And that is not now.'

'Sorry, sir', said the barman. 'But the lady at the other end of the bar is the RSM's wife and she says to close the bar.'

All four of us looked around in amazement. It was then that I recognised one of the ladies as the RSM's wife but what was she doing in the Mess on her own? Under normal Warrant Officers and Sergeants' Mess rules a wife, or partner to be politically correct, can only enter the Mess when accompanied by her serving spouse. In many Messes a member's partner cannot sit at the bar, let alone buy drinks.

'Corporal, you tell the RSM's wife that I am the senior serving member here and I want the bar to stay open.'

So off trotted the barman to speak to the lady concerned. While he was out of hearing range, the RQMS let us know that he had fallen out with the RSM's wife over some minor point and that he was not too chuffed that she was in the Mess at all but, so as not to antagonise the situation, had refrained from saying anything.

'What is she doing in here on her own?' one of my fellow drinkers asked.

We were informed that she was already in the bar when the RQMS arrived so to save any further hassle between them, he had said nothing, even when he noted that she had a guest with her, which was another Mess taboo she had transgressed.

'Sorry sir, but the RSM's wife says that she considers that you have had enough drink and that as the RSM's wife she wants the bar closed.'

This was just too much for the RQMS who stormed up to the bar, grabbed the RSM's wife off her barstool and marched her to the nearest exit. Screaming all sorts of unmentionable things she was unceremoniously bundled out of the Mess into the car park. The female guest who had remained seated at the bar waited until the RQMS returned and then fled the Mess.

The RQMS rejoined us at the bar, where we stayed until the early hours and nothing was mentioned between us about the incident.

Next morning the RQMS was waiting outside the RSM's office when he arrived for work. Once inside the RSM explained that he had urgently wanted to see the RQMS about the previous evening's events as his wife had re-enacted them in rather hysterical and full graphic detail. After a long chat the RSM explained that his wife was becoming far too pretentious, was a real pain and embarrassment to him. He finally thanked the RQMS for his actions, they shook hands and that evening went out for a few beers.

Crooks, Vagabonds and Thieves

One thing that anyone reading this, or trying to understand service life, must come to terms with is that the Army is only a small microcosm of civilian life with all its inevitable faults. The services have their fair share of personnel engaged in incestuous behaviour, cross-dressers, assaults, wife-swapping and spouse beating, drunkenness and drugs and, of course, theft. Contrary to what some people would have you believe, there are homosexuals in the services and these can be found in all ranks, commissioned and non-commissioned, and in all trades and units, from storeman to special forces and from infantry to intelligence.

I well remember a drugs raid that took place in my unit just prior to a leave period. The RMP, and their Special Investigations Branch, had received information that drugs were in the junior ranks accommodation. After a thorough search no illegal substances were found, but one interesting find did result in a unit investigation.

In one of the lad's lockers a small sports bag was found to contain ladies' underwear and clothing, plus cosmetics and a wig. The soldier concerned stated that he had found the bag on a train and was holding it prior to handing it in at the local railway station as lost property. Under pressure of further investigation he confessed that the bag and its contents were his and that he spent his weekends and leave periods in London as a transvestite. After medical and psychiatric examinations, it was assumed that the lad did not engage in any homosexual activities while dressed as a female and he was offered counselling. However, the matter had become common knowledge among his peers and to save him and the unit any further embarrassment the lad was granted an administrative discharge from the Army.

Another case that I can recall involved a sergeant who worked in the unit quartermasters' store. Several reports were received from soldiers living in the junior ranks accommodation that items of military equipment and civilian possessions had gone missing. The unit hierarchy were convinced that it was one of the soldiers but were confounded when it was revealed that items had disappeared from locked rooms and individual bunks.

One afternoon the RQMS went looking for his sergeant who was supposed to be in the accommodation checking a reported water leak. As the RQMS entered the building he literally bumped into the sergeant who had arms full of uniform items and sleeping bags. Not impressed by the SNCO's answers as to what he was doing with these items, he escorted the man back to the QM's office, where he was interrogated further. Asked to empty out his pockets he produced a full set of duplicate keys that would give access to all the accommodation rooms and bunks.

The QM decided that he would contact the RMP, to have them investigate this further, and was told that a police patrol would be sent to his office in about one hour. The sergeant then pleaded with the QM for permission to return to his married quarters to inform his wife what was happening and that he might be late back from work. Unfortunately the QM agreed to this and the man disappeared, unescorted to his home. He was still absent when the police arrived and they were not too impressed when told what had happened. They immediately went around to the sergeant's house to interview him and bring him back to the unit lines.

When a full investigation was completed, some illegal equipment was found at the man's house and he admitted that he had had the duplicate keys made so that he could gain access to the accommodation. Unfortunately, the case had to be dropped on technicalities, in part due to the fact that the QM had allowed him to leave the scene of the crime, possibly giving the sergeant time to get rid of any incriminating evidence.

The last time I met this man he had been commissioned and was posted to the Far East in the rank of major.

Such nefarious activities are not solely carried out by enlisted troops; officers have been known to participate in similar schemes. One of the more ridiculous scams concerned a major who was court martialled for fraud after he was caught submitting claims for board school allowances for his three children. Unfortunately for the officer concerned, some eagle-eyed individual noticed that one of the children was only four months old.

There's Some Strange Folk About

A fellow Junior NCO had been caught outside a local girls' school offering the pupils sweets and rides in his car. After his appearance before the civil judiciary, where he was found guilty of a public order offence, he was dealt with by the military. At his court martial he was found guilty of some offence or other and he was reduced to the ranks and given an immediate disciplinary posting to a Mediterranean country.

The unit orderly sergeant and I were detailed to box up the contents of his bunk and hand them to the QM for freighting to the lad's next unit. When we opened his lockers we were stunned by what we found.

Apart from the usual civilian and military possessions you would expect to find, we also encountered a 14-inch electronic vibrator, an assortment of rubber and leather clothing (male and female), various whips, handcuffs and chains, and a large collection of hardcore porn magazines that seemed to cover every possible sexual practice imaginable.

I only hope that when the boxes and their contents lists were presented at Customs they did not give the wrong impression of this otherwise upstanding member of Her Majesty's Forces.

Cocktails, My Dear?

During the latter stages of my military career I became emotionally and physically attached to a female junior officer. Now, this breaks with all the protocols of good service life and such things are wholly frowned upon by the powers that be. It just wasn't cricket for an officer to get involved with an enlisted troop. Plus at about the same time one or two scandals had hit the front pages of the tabloid press.

None the less we carried on this relationship and were always extremely careful not to display affections should we meet while in uniform. Having said that, my girlfriend was rather adamant that I attend a cocktail party, with her, at her Officers' Mess. Fortunately her Mess was in another garrison and she insisted that there would be no one there who would recognise me. Just in case, we agreed a suitable pseudonym and employment.[47]

The fateful evening arrived and suitably decked out in black tie I arrived at the Officers' Mess on the arm of my loved one. Everything was going swimmingly until a senior female officer, who was doing a poor impersonation of Madam Host, joined our small group. Having been introduced to her, she asked the customary few inane questions and was just about to wander to the next group when she stopped dead in her tracks and turned back to me.

'May I just ask why you are wearing your watch on your right wrist?' she blurted out.[48]

Having to think quickly on my feet I came to the most suitable answer I could in the time allowed.

'Why, yes of course', I replied. 'It's because it is an automatic watch and I wear it that way so that it winds itself up every time I go to bed.'

'Oh! How very interesting,' she continued, 'I knew it would have something to do with you job.'

She had walked away a few steps before she realised the true meaning of what I had said. She blushed and stated in no uncertain terms that such a person was not the correct type of gentleman to be involved with one of her nice girls. Whereupon she asked me to leave.

It also ended my-eight month romance.

Regimental Dinners

British Army Regimental Messes are a splendid military tradition that should never be lost. They are steeped in military history and rituals. Whether it be the Officers' or Sergeants' Mess, they are the envy of every other military organisation worldwide, with many countries emulating this finest of military establishments. Within this framework it is well accepted that the Warrant Officers' or Sergeants' Mess is the true powerhouse of any unit. Without its backing, customs, and practices, no unit can function correctly. A happy and well-run Sergeants' Mess will undoubtedly lead to a happy and well-run unit.

There are many fascinating and deeply historical procedures and rules within each regiment and corps, which are best seen in the daily life of the Mess. None more so than a Regimental Dinner Night in the Sergeants' Mess. But even these can go awry on some occasions.

In nearly all the Messes that I went into, it was standard procedure that once you sat down for the meal no one was allowed to leave the table, especially not to use the toilet. This would include the lady members as well if there were any. I have known people to have themselves catheterised prior to a dinner rather than incur the wrath of the Mess Presiding Member, by having to leave the table for a personal emergency.[49] I have also seen members quickly remove their Mess jackets, jump up and pretend to be waiters so that they can sneak out of the room.

I well remember one nine-course dinner that seemed to go on and on. A person sitting opposite me covertly asked one of the waiters to open a large window just behind his seat. He then quickly climbed through and went off to use the toilet. Fortunately no one on the top table noticed his disappearance, but the people around his now vacant seat decided to set him up when he returned. Quietly and with minimum fuss his chair was removed as was all his cutlery and place setting. Finally, the diners each side of his space then closed ranks so that there was nowhere for him to return to.

Ten or fifteen minutes later, a head appeared at the open window and with a howl of laughter he noticed what had happened. Unperturbed, he disappeared again only to walk out from the kitchen serving area a few minutes later. Unable to find a suitable chair he had dragged out a large blue plastic bin and a handful of cutlery. Some on the top table now glared across as he positioned himself at the end of one of the tables using the bin as a seat. He certainly caught their eyes when, due to either the bin collapsing or the amount of wine he had consumed, he fell off the bin onto the floor. To make matters worse the bin was full of flour and this went everywhere. I believe this cost him a Christmas duty, a £200 donation to a local charity and case of port for the RSM.

On another occasion the Mess had invited a prominent Member of Parliament as guest speaker. As he stood to address the members, one of the sergeants slid off his chair and began crawling under the tables towards the top table. Just as the speaker was getting to the punchline of a joke, he let out a scream and jumped back from where he stood. Much to the amusement of all present, which fortunately included our guest speaker, the sergeant had bitten him on the ankle.

During yet another dinner we were honoured by the presence of one of the original officers of the regiment, now a retired and rather gin-sodden old brigadier. As the port flowed and after an introduction by the Presiding Member, he stood to regale us with his exploits. Regrettably he could not follow the line of his own story and would repeat the same thing time and again. As a matter of fact it became embarrassing as he waffled on and on about inane and unrelated topics. Finally, when everyone had totally lost interest, one of the warrant officers banged the table with a candlestick and stood up. After thanking the speaker for his excellent talk he then asked the gentleman to sit down so that we could adjourn to the bar.

Regimental Dinners were often used to 'dine out' Mess members when they were either posted out of the unit or when they came to the end of their military careers. I remember hearing about one such dinner, which was used to dine out a member who was leaving the Army. He was also renowned for his sense of humour. After a fellow member had made a short oration extolling the virtues of his character and thanking him on behalf of the Mess and the Army for his dedication and service, he replied by jumping on the table and mounting a skateboard. He then rode the skateboard down the table, jumped off the end and disappeared out of the Mess never to return.

I also remember a Regimental Dinner that nearly exploded into a fistfight. The dinner was a tri-service affair, with the Army element mainly made up from two regiments. The Presiding Member for the dinner was a garrison sergeant major, who hailed from a Scottish regiment.

The dinner went well until the Loyal Toasts at the end of the meal. The PMC stood and asked all to be upstanding for the Loyal Toast to Her Majesty the Queen. What the GSM had failed to remember was that the Royal Navy never stand for the Loyal Toast and that one of the regiments present (a Guards unit) never does a Loyal Toast as their loyalty to the sovereign is never in doubt.[50] When the GSM and a few others noticed that some people had not stood for the toast, he went ballistic and started shouting at the senior RN and Guards personnel calling them all sorts of names and disgraces. It was only when he was informed of these long, standing regimental and service traditions that he calmed down and the potential fight was averted.

Special Forces

During my military career the sector of Special Forces greatly increased. The term now seems to encompass not only the Special Air Service and Special Boat Squadron but numerous other units and formations including Path Finder units, Army Marine personnel, Intelligence units and even some Royal Air Force squadrons. I was fortunate enough to spend nearly half my service career working directly with such units.

Hence this section of the book will deal with incidents pertaining to all so-called 'Special Forces' units.

First Day in an Airborne Unit

Dressed for arrival at my new unit in No.2 Dress Uniform, No.1 Dress hat and best boots, I was shown into the old Victorian barrack block that was the unit's headquarters. Having been instructed to report to the orderly sergeant's office, which was on the first floor, I struggled up the stairs with all my worldly goods stuffed into an Army suitcase, Army holdall and Army kitbag. Nearing the top I was suddenly confronted by what I would conservatively call the largest and meanest looking person I had ever seen. He stood at the top of the stairs, hands on hips, red beret on his head and caused a total eclipse of the sun.[51]

I had been told that a real Para is someone who is 200lbs of airborne fury, can chew nails, spit sparks and jump out of iron birds. He can run from Land's End to John O'Groats non-stop with a 60lb bergen on his back. He drinks like a fish and will fight anyone who crosses his path. The apparition in front of me certainly looked like a real Para.

When he asked what I thought I was doing entering the hallowed domain of an airborne unit, I sheepishly replied that I had been posted into the unit and was heading for the orderly sergeant's office.

'Well,' he commanded in a lucid and cogent voice, 'as of now you are supposedly a member of this airborne unit' and, referring to my No.1 Dress peaked cap, he continued, 'and we don't wear f***ing crap hats in the Airborne.'[52] With one swift and easy movement he removed my cap, ripped the peak off it and flattened what remained by smashing his highly polished boot down on it.

'Report immediately to the unit clothing store', he bellowed. 'Get yourself some proper headdress and report back to my office in ten minutes.'

When I finally reported into the orderly sergeant's office, I was sweating profusely, my uniform was creased and crumpled, and on my head was a brand new red beret about the size of a helicopter landing zone.

After the customary new arrivals interview with the CO, 2i/c, adjutant and the RSM, I received a full in-depth brief on the unit from the orderly sergeant, who this time managed to refrain from ripping my headdress off and jumping on it. After being shown to my capacious fifteen-man barrack room accommodation I was informed where and when to parade so that I could meet the Physical Training Instructor, who would be in charge of my life for the next few weeks.

His name was 'Big' Jim and I soon saw why. He was over 6ft tall, had muscles in places I didn't know people had places and there wasn't an ounce of fat on him. His well-tanned and toned body just fitted into his immaculately tailored uniform. With his Airborne Forces red beret on his head he looked every inch a proud and admirable member of the Parachute Brigade.

On parade were four students, all of us were first-time attendees at Unit Pre-Parachute Selection Training.[53] After the customary introductions we were given ten minutes to change uniform and were off on our first 'speed march' which thankfully was only eighteen miles carrying a 40lb bergen!!

Returning to the unit, we did some loosing-off exercises, which consisted of fifty push-ups while still wearing our bergens, fifty sit-ups and sprinting on the spot for a minute. Big Jim had done everything we had without the courtesy of breaking into even a slight sweat and he seemed rather vexed that we looked somewhat knackered. After a briefing on what the next day held, a well-earned tea meal and preparing my kit for the next day I crawled into bed. With stiff legs and my whole body aching I lay there thinking what the hell had I let myself in for.

I later found out that at roughly the same time that I lapsed into a dead beat coma, Big Jim was finishing his daily two hours of pumping iron and was setting off on a ten-mile road run.

You Called Me What?

During my second week in the Airborne we were called into the Quartermaster's yard to be instructed on the correct handling procedures for the No.1 Burner. This petrol-fuelled fiery monster was the main piece of equipment used by chefs to cook with while in the field. Unfortunately, a young soldier on a training exercise in Germany had been killed using one of these, when he had over-pressurised the fuel container and the safety nipple had blown off and shot through his chest, killing him almost immediately.

The QM's Staff Sergeant, or CQMS[54] as he was known, gathered us around and went through the correct way to refill, prime, pressurise and ignite the burner. Having completed this he looked around the assembled mass and asked for a volunteer to run through the whole thing again to prove that we understood his instructions. As no one stepped forward (good military men never volunteer for anything) the CQMS picked out Big Jim, the Unit Pre-Para instructor. Commenting that, as Big Jim was possibly the least intelligent of those present, if he could do it then everyone else must have understood the lecture.

Big Jim started correctly and was just about to pressurise the fuel container when what the CQMS had said struck him. Not too impressed in being called the thickness of the bunch Big Jim picked up the fully fuelled burner with one hand and swung it at the CQMS, who having just managed to duck the blow, ran off and locked himself into one of the storerooms. It took several minutes for Big Jim to calm down and to hand over the burner, which he was still waving above his head as he beat on the storeroom door.

Dun's River Falls or Does It?

After successfully passing 'P' Company and living long enough to
qualify for my Parachute wings, I was rewarded with a trip to Jamaica.
This was a real culture shock from my 'real' Army days and I thoroughly enjoyed it. For the most part we were located at a small tented
camp up in the Blue Mountains but when not practising battle tactics
with the Jamaican Defence Force, we toured the island looking at the
hot spots and mixing with tourists that had forked out thousands to
get there, while we were being paid to suffer the place.

We visited all the famous tourist places and spent many a day on the
beaches at Montego Bay, Ocho Rios and Port Antonio. Errol Flynn's
house was invaded and a suitable quantity of rum and beer demolished.

After a morning playing soldiers, some of us went off to do a spot of
rafting on one of the local rivers. You could hire a ready-made
bamboo raft and someone to pole you along but we decided to build
our own. So we set to work with machetes, cutting down bamboo poles
and lashing them together to form our trusty rafts. Some of the local
lads gathered watching us, some offered to build the things for us (for
a price), but generally they just sat laughing at our attempts. Not to be
put off, we persevered and hours later were ready for the launching
ceremony.

We great pride and fanfare we pushed the rafts out into the river.
Only to watch them go straight to the bottom. Once the howls of
laughter from our watchers died down they explained that there are
two types of bamboo and only one that floats.

Accommodation

As a young lance corporal in an Airborne unit, I was initially pleased
to find that I had been allocated one of a row of four individual bunks
on the top floor of our accommodation block. This soon turned out to
be a millstone around my neck as I had the habit of leaving the door
key inside whenever I ventured out. After a month or two, I had been
fined several hundred pounds for smashing in the door, usually on my
return from a night out in the local bars.

So on the next occasion that this happened I was determined not to waste my hard-earned pay. Climbing up through the roof space and onto the flat roof I lowered myself over the edge of the block and while hanging from my fingertips I used my feet to slide the window open. Employing all my Para training I swung into the room and rolled across the carpet to break my fall-a job well done.

However, I had made a fatal error in calculating which was my room. This was dramatically brought home to me when the once sleeping occupant of the room jumped out of bed and physically removed me from his bunk.

On Officer Commanding's Orders next day I was once again fined £50 for damage done to Her Majesty's Government's property, after I had had to resort to kicking open the door to my bunk so that I could get some sleep.

Plastic Paras

A new RSM was posted in to the unit while I was with the Paras. He was to be with us for a short tour prior to getting his officer's commission. To make things worse he had never served with the Airborne before. The RSM became a real pain in the backside and was possibly the most hated person I encountered in my service career. Lads returning from a night out at the pub would regularly take a short detour past his house and scratch the paintwork off his car, or rip off the wing mirrors or windscreen wipers.

At the end of the year and just prior to the unit going on Christmas/New Year leave we had an informal unit 'smoker' or party in the unit bar. The Commanding Officer, an excellent and well-respected gentleman, had paid for a few barrels of beer as his reward to the unit for an all-round successful year. Towards the finish of the party the CO stood on a table and gave a great speech about how well the unit had done, both militarily and on the sports field. He wished us the best for the future and seasonal greetings. He finished off by stating that he looked forward to seeing us all in the New Year. With three cheers from the lads, the CO drank up and left.

The RSM, just to prove what a prat he was, decided to emulate the CO and make a speech too. Unfortunately, he pitched the whole thing wrong and to show what we thought of him we all turned our backs to him. This made his blood boil, and he screamed threats and recriminations at us. He finished by telling us to ensure that we all returned on time, with proper haircuts and that the first muster parade of the New Year would be in full parade dress (No.2 Dress). He then left and we carried on with the party.

The RSM went to his office to clear his desk prior to the holidays. However, on the desk was a small parcel. Neatly wrapped in Christmas paper and tied with a silver bow, it had a label on it 'To the RSM, from the lads of the unit'. With tears welling up in his eyes he opened his present only to find a box of Airfix miniature plastic paratroopers and a note stating 'RSM. F**k this lot around while we're on leave'.

Lost Weapons

Our RSM could not parachute into an exercise area like the rest of the unit, as for some godforsaken reason the MoD had posted him to the Paras when he was not currently, or ever had been, Para trained. So he had to be driven there and meet us on the Dropping Zone (DZ). He also had no idea whatsoever about being a field soldier and these combined to make the unit a bit of a laughing stock with other Airborne units.

Thus, while on an Airborne exercise, he took advantage of the fact that most of our officers had been called away to Brigade HQ for a tactical briefing, to further humiliate us by holding a full unit parade in a forest clearing. While the rest of the brigade defended our perimeter against possible enemy action, we had to form up in three ranks and strip down our weapons so that he could inspect them for cleanliness.

Our senior ranks and warrant officers, plus the few junior officers left in location, told him in no uncertain terms that this was not the done thing and that the rest of the brigade were more than a little amused with such antics. But he insisted, he was our RSM and he could do what he wanted.

Parade over, we returned to tactical duties and night fell over the area. Next morning we were woken by the RSM wandering around, rather sheepishly asking if anyone had his personal weapon. He had it when he went to sleep last night but somehow it had disappeared from beside his sleeping bag.

The RSM never found the weapon and never got his commission. As far as I know the weapon is still buried on the training area and the two SNCOs who buried it completed full and rewarding military careers.

A Press-Up Too Far

One extremely fit Airborne warrior, who epitomised the saying 'I can't read or write but I can lift heavy weights', had damaged his shoulder during a parachute jump into France. On his return to the UK the corporal tried to resume his punishing fitness routine but was hampered by a recurring shoulder pain. So off he goes to see the Regimental Medical Officer (RMO).

Asked by the doctor what the problem was, he tried to explain but was unable to adequately describe it due to his lack of medical and anatomical understanding and of a basic grasp of the spoken word. The RMO, while being fully sympathetic to the man's plight, could not accurately pinpoint the problem. As a result he asked the NCO what sort of activity aggravated the problem and was informed that such exercises as press-ups did this. So the RMO told the soldier to carry out a few of the exercises, in his examination room, until the pain appeared and meanwhile the doctor would finish some paperwork on his desk. After a time the corporal stood up and stated that the pain had returned.

It was during the subsequent meticulous examination, and after no significant musculoskeletal problems were found, that the RMO asked how many press-ups had been achieved. The corporal stated 140. Accordingly, the doctor instructed him that the prognosis was straight-forward. He was to simply cut down on the number of press-ups and the pain would ease with time.

Dinner for Four

At one unit we had just had a noticeably effeminate cook posted in, in fact his wrists were so limp he had a job tying his bootlaces. He was of

French Canadian extraction, which unfortunately gave him a rather gauche accent (suspiciously, some thought it 'cute').[55] For obvious reasons he was not Para trained, but was supposedly renowned for his catering expertise, and especially for small parties.

It was pure coincidence that at a time when this cook was working in the main unit cookhouse, one of my chums obtained permission to go shooting on a local estate. So we arranged for this cook, at a price, to prepare a small dinner party for four of us and the main course would be whatever was bagged on the next shoot. The following Saturday, and after three brace of pheasant had been shot out of the sky, we sat down in the dining hall at a small candlelit table bedecked with silver service.

The starter was a very nice prawn cocktail, followed by an excellent lime sorbet, both enhanced by a suitable wine. After these were cleared away an array of vegetables appeared, along with three dishes containing a selection of rice dishes. To much fanfare the cook entered with a large tureen, which he placed in the centre of the table. To our applause and thanks, he lifted the lid to reveal his culinary surprise.

And what a surprise it was. He had slaved over a hot stove for many hours to produce this gastronomic pièce de résistance-pheasant curry.

Log Run Around Town

One of the great things about the Special Forces is their esprit de corps and camaraderie. This includes a great deal of social bonding or, to put it another way, partying, drinking and fighting. As a young soldier in the Parachute Brigade I would often get involved in such pastimes. In fact, it was damn near compulsory.

It became known throughout the lower classes of the brigade that an inter-unit log race was to be held the next Saturday morning and the route would be through the centre of the town. Each unit would supply a log (or telegraph pole to give it its correct description) and eight men to carry it. Fancy dress was, as usual, optional. The local police and Military Police were informally warned of this just before the race started and they were only too willing to stop any traffic along the three-mile route.[56]

At the appointed time and place seven teams assembled. Each log was tested to make certain that it was of sufficient weight (i.e. had not been hollowed out) and the positioning of each carrying strap was checked. At the drop of the barmaid's knickers, they were off, down the street from the roundabout to the Post Office, turning right and up the hill. Watched by many bemused civilians and closely followed by more than just a few drunken Airborne soldiers, the teams vied for first position. Always careful not to damage property or cars parked on the side of the road, the teams raced along the centre of the street.

Turning right into a shopping precinct the teams brushed aside anyone too slow to dart out of the way. However, instead of continuing on to the end of the street and turning right, the lead team decided to veer through Woolworth's. Skilfully passing the sweet counter, the record and cassette displays and checkout, they emerged back out onto the main road. The odd scream and muffled obscenity was heard as the other six teams of sweating and vaguely out of breath warriors manhandled their logs through the store as well.

Racing down the hill to the roundabout and the start/finish line, others cheered on the teams from their units; even the odd civilian joined in. Once over the line the logs were quickly dumped behind a wooden fence and the teams vanished into the local hostelries to replace essential body fluids.

Stamp Run

Another event that occurred on a frequent basis was the Stamp Run. This required even-numbered teams to form into queues at the bar. The front man of each team would then drink a pint of beer as fast as possible, or 'boat race' as it was called. Once the glass was empty he put it upside down on the bar and raced out of the pub. After sprinting 200 metres along the road to the Post Office, he was then required to purchase a single stamp from the vending machine on the wall, stick it to his forehead and dash back to the pub. To ensure fair play, non-partisan observers were deployed along the route. Once back in the bar, he had to drink another pint of beer before the next member of the team was allowed to start. The winning team were treated to copious amounts of drinks purchased by the other teams.

Many a bemused shopper would stop on a Saturday afternoon to watch the frantic activities of fancy-dressed or semi-naked males hurtling up and down one of the town's main streets.

The Roundabout Siege

One fine summer's day, a Saturday I think, the centre of town was brought to a standstill. Several of the brigade units had decided to storm the large roundabout that signified the line between the military garrison and the civilian town and to hold it against all odds. That included the police, both civil and military, and any other such authority deemed enemy of the day.

Flowerbeds had been dug up and converted into battle trenches, wire and other barricades were erected at the perimeter and nearly fifty soldiers in various forms of disguise and dress were ready for action. First on the scene were the civil police who tried to talk the defenders off the roundabout. Having no luck they called in the Military Police. They tried their usual patter of cajolement then heavy-handed bullyboy threats but the troops were not ready to throw in the towel just yet. To make things worse (for the police) a large crowd was forming and shouts of encouragement went up for the lads defending the roundabout.

Mounted police were then sent in but could not get up on to the elevated roundabout through the maze of wire and barricades. Finally the local fire brigade arrived and set to with high-pressure hoses to blast the troops into submission. All the same, as the barriers were slowly eroded and the heroic defenders had to evacuate their trenches, a large contingent of soldiers, in civilian clothing, rushed forward and engulfed the now sought after individuals who were then spirited away out of the reach of the Orwellian authorities. Unable to catch their men, the police were just grateful that the roundabout was vacated and they could finally open the roads again.

None the less the day was not completely finished. One of the inter-lopers had survived the siege and climbed up a nearby lamp-post. Halfway up the concrete post were large flower baskets and our friend was now sitting in one of these. The police, using fire brigade ladders, tried to haul him down but he was screaming that if they removed him they would be murderers, as the eggs he had laid would cool, not hatch and the unborn chicks would die. To make matters worse he had handcuffed himself to the lamp-post.

Understanding the futility of it, the police retreated. As they did so, he undid the handcuff, climbed down and to loud applause, calmly wandered into a local pub for a well-earned beer.

Heads it's a Horse

After a quiet Saturday lunchtime drinking session many of the off-duty soldiers would wander into a park near the centre of town. (Please remember that in those days the pubs used to close in the afternoon.) Some lads would carry on drinking from cans or bottles, while other would have a quick siesta on the grass and prepare themselves for the evening session.

On this particular occasion and for some unknown reason, police surrounded the park. I think the local populace must have complained about this regular event. To totally overdo things the Military Police (MP) sent in their Mounted Section, to eject the drinkers and sleepers. Most of us just got up and walked away but some of the others became rather belligerent at their treatment.

One rather unrefined and legendary chap was, I remember, fast asleep when a mounted MP rode up to him. Using some fancy equine trick he got the horse to knock the man in the back with its hoof. The soldier just simply rolled over and went back to sleep. When the mounted MP did this again the soldier actually woke up. Instantly assessing the situation he stared up at the MP and informed him that if the horse did that again the police officer would be extremely sorry. Sitting some five or six feet up on his horse the MP must have felt secure and treated this as nothing more than an intoxicated threat. So he had the horse knock the soldier again. Instantly the soldier was on his feet and facing the horse. Reminding the MP of his warning, he quickly and rather expertly executed a decisive head-butt on the horse. The look of sheer astonishment on the MP's face as his horse tumbled to the ground under him will be with me for ever.

Early Morning Rise

After just a year in the Paras, having passed my Assistant Instructor of Physical Training course over two years before, I was installed as the head of unit routine fitness training. I was actually the junior of the three PT Instructors in the unit. But of the other two, one was full-time with the unit's Pre-Para Selection team and the other was on detachment in Canada.

The day of this auspicious elevation into the management of the unit I was collared by several of the old hands and informed that the RSM was planning to reschedule the daily fitness training to start at 0700 hours for one hour, followed by breakfast at 0830 hours and unit muster parade at 0900 hours. They all advised me that this was illegal, as according to Queen's Regulations for the Army, breakfast was officially the first parade of any working day. Unable, for some reason, to find a copy of these regulations I reluctantly asked to see the RSM about this and other training matters.

After exchanging the usual pleasantries that a lance corporal does when on interview with his RSM, I broached the subject of Daily Fitness Training and mentioned that I understood that the new schedule could be problematic. Having listened to my understanding of the issue, the RSM promised to look into this; after discussing the other matters I was dismissed and returned to my place of work.

Later that day I was amazed to read that the RSM had indeed changed the timings for morning parades. Fitness Training was still at 0700 hours, however, breakfast was now at 0600 hours and muster parade at 0830 hours.

So that most of the single lads did not have to get up for breakfast at 0600 hours and to combat the short time between the end of PT and muster parade, it became normal practice for us to get takeaway meals the night before and leave them on the barrack room radiators. This ensured that we had something warm to eat as we hastily changed out of sports kit into working dress in time for parade. Some even invested in microwave ovens, while others just starved until the mid-morning break when they could get pies, rolls and sandwiches from the NAAFI.

Welcome Home

Due to appalling weather our airborne exercise was cancelled and we were sent back to barracks early. En route a plan was hatched whereby one of the married lads would hand in our weapons to the armoury, while we quickly got our drinking clothes on. We would then head down town for a night on the pop, via the married quarters so that the married lads could change into civvies and join us.

All went well until we got to one of the married quarters and the lad did not have his key. We stood outside his house as he rang the doorbell and expected his wife to answer. However, we were all stunned when the door opened and a semi-naked male asked us what we wanted.

'I want to come in', pleaded the surprised husband.

'Sorry mate,' came the reply 'she has four here at present and she can't handle any more.'

Quick as a flash it dawned on us what was going on, so we pushed past the doorman and stormed into the house. Our comrade in arms was slightly more than flabbergasted to find his wife in bed with two men, while one of the others was still getting undressed and the man who had answered the door had finished his business and was on his way out.

Having physically removed the visitors, we also left the house so that the husband could have 'a chat' with his wife. We were yet again amazed when after only five or ten minutes of loud discussion the husband rejoined us, having changed into his party rags, and insisted that we all head to the nearest public house.

It later emerged that he had given his wife only one option to his problem. She had to be out of the married quarters, lock stock and barrel, by the time he came back from the pub or she could expect to spend a few days as a resident of the local hospital.

Wedded Bliss

The unit bar of any military formation is usually the centre of out-of-hour's entertainment and this is especially so in Special Forces units where the ethos of 'live hard, play hard' would be the norm.

A party, in the bar, had been arranged as the stag night for one of the unit characters who was finally taking the leap into marital harmony. It was well attended and as the drinks flowed it wasn't long before the groom was suffering from the effects of copious amounts of alcohol; the fact that his drinks were spiked with almost pure alcohol may have had something to do with this.

As the evening drew to a close the groom put up very little resistance when he was pinned to the floor, stripped naked and mummified from head to foot in plaster of paris bandages, no body area being spared except for his eyes and nose so that he could see and breathe. Once the bandages had set hard we carried him out of the bar and loaded him into a Land Rover. He was then driven around the garrison to disorientate him before being unloaded and laid at the side of the road.

In fact he was just out of view of a unit guardroom the other side of the garrison. Unable to move he had to lie there as soldiers staggered past on their way back from the pub. Eventually the guards were informed of his presence and he ended up being taken to the local casualty department where the plaster of paris was cut off. I never did find out how he explained his predicament to the hospital staff or how he got back home without money or clothes.

The next time I saw him was at the wedding the following day when he surprised his bride, and the in-laws, by appearing totally hairless.

Sole Jumps

Seven of the unit had been detailed to carry out a night-time, clean fatigue, parachute descent onto Salisbury Plain, so we drove down to RAF Lyneham in good time.[57] On our arrival it became obvious that we were the only unit supplying personnel for this task and wondered what was going to happen. The RAF detail was for five Hercules C130 aircraft to carry out Streamer Training over the Channel for three hours before routing back to Lyneham via the dropping zone (DZ) on Salisbury Plain. This meant that the aircraft would fly in tight formation, one behind the other, over the Channel and at low level. The lead C130 would have a nice time of it, while the slipstream of the plane in front and the air currents coming up from the sea would buffet the following planes. Airsickness was the order of the day.

As there were only a total of seven parachutists we were given the option of either all out of one plane or one parachutist out of each of the first three planes and two out of the each of the last two planes. The choice was difficult as the three-hour, low-level flight would be much more comfortable in the first plane but the opportunity to do a single-person static line descent out of your own aircraft was too much for us. It turned out that I would be in the third aircraft in the stream of five.

I had to draw and fit my own parachute, manifest myself onto the plane's cargo sheets, do my own safety checks, and warn myself about refusing to jump.[58] For takeoff I was allowed to sit in the cockpit and once the low-level flying began I went into the cargo area and had a sleep. At the appointed time the Air Loadmaster, who was to act as my dispatcher, woke me up and told me to refit my 'chute. As we started the run-in I was given the choice of which door to use, starboard or port, so I chose my favourite, which was a port-side exit.

Just before Action Stations was called I stood halfway down the plane facing the port door, when the red light came on I started walking towards it. Just as I reached the door the green light came on so I just carried on walking and dropped out into the night sky.

It was really eerie to be the only one hanging there in the night sky; usually you have other parachutists to worry about as they may drift into you and cause all sorts of problems, including collapsing your 'chute. The landing went well and we all met up on the DZ without incident. On the way home we wondered what the taxpayers would think if they knew how much our jolly parachute jumps had just cost.

Tree Jump

At the start of a large NATO exercise in northern Germany I was among the first wave of British Paras to jump into the area. It was a night jump supposedly into a very large clear valley, but for some reason the glorious RAF missed the dropping zone by miles and the majority of us landed in trees.

Once my parachute and I had settled in the top of the trees I quickly remembered my training. Unhooking my reserve parachute I climbed out of the harness and started a slow and very careful descent of the tree. It was pitch dark and had been raining so the bark and branches were slimy. Getting to the bottom branch I still could not see the forest floor, so I decided to stay where I was until it got lighter as dawn approached.

Perched on the branch and with my back to the tree trunk I could hear an array of rather untactical banter from many others in a similar predicament. I found out that my section sergeant was in the next tree and he had inadvertently dropped his reserve 'chute.

As dawn broke I could see that I was some eighty to ninety feet from the ground and that even if I deployed my reserve 'chute as a means of getting down I would still have a fair way to drop. So I stayed where I was. Across the forest I could see a chap who had carried out this drill and had climbed down the nylon lines but had for some reason ended up inside the parachute and could neither climb back out nor cut his way out as he did not have a knife with him.

As I sat chatting to my section sergeant we could hear a fellow tree jumper being coaxed to jump down off his perch. The person was obviously a British officer but even this did not sway the chap to follow his orders.

'Come on lad', shouted the officer. 'You've only got a few feet to jump. Remember feet and knees together with a sharp Para roll on landing and you'll be OK. Now on my count of three. One, two, three, jump.'

'No way, I'll break my bloody neck-sir', replied the soldier.

'Look, it's clear of stumps and other problems, soft wet earth, nothing to worry about.'

'OK, OK', stammered the soldier.

'One, two, three, jump', called the officer. 'Oh!! Come along now-you are a trained Para after all. Here we go again. Ready, one, two, three, jump.'

The next thing we heard was a scream, sharply followed by a loud call for a medic. Shame really, as all the medics around were hanging in trees.

The local village fire brigade had been called out to help but the only ladders they could use were wooden and nowhere near long enough.

Eight hours after landing in my tree I had to climb back up the branches to be winched out by a German police helicopter. What a way to start a multi-national NATO exercise.

French Parachute Training

In the lead-up to 16 Parachute Brigade becoming 5 Airborne Brigade, one of the Pathfinder units was to be disbanded. As a finale the unit went off to France and I joined it for this final exercise. As part of the training we were to gain our French Para wings by completing a series of parachute jumps from various French aircraft and using their parachutes. After six descents we reached the final day and the final qualifying jump. The weather had closed in and it looked as though time had beaten us. Nevertheless, we boarded the aircraft and took off. Circling the DZ we could see that the wind was well and truly howling and that the cloud-base had come down.

The French dispatchers and the ground safety officer were about to call the whole thing off when our OC demanded to speak to them over the plane's radio system. He pleaded with them and reiterated that this would be the unit's last ever parachute jump together and that it meant a lot to all of us (or so he thought) that we complete the course and the exercise as a unit. Not wishing to disappoint us they reluctantly agreed to allow the jump to continue and wished us well.

When I hit the ground I was dragged for a hundred yards or so, before I could collapse the canopy and stand up. All around there were bodies bouncing across the DZ and several were obviously injured. The final toll was: out of the 44 personnel that jumped 11 had to be treated in the medical centre. The most serious injury was the OC, who had unfortunately landed in a tree and broken his leg.

German Parachute Training

Not long after gaining my French Parachute wings I was off to Bavaria in Germany to have a go at their parachute training course. The jumps were made from a Transall C160, very much like the Hercules C130 we used, except it had only two engines, which made it much quieter inside than the Hercules. The other difference was that it had a siren alarm that sounded when it was time to exit the aircraft. On the C130 you have a series of red and green lights and on the green light you followed your leader out the door. If a siren sounds in the Hercules it means that the plane is about to ditch, so when the siren sounded on our first jump from a C160, there were some very nervous parachutists hurrying through the doors.

Another difference between our military parachute techniques is that we are dispatched out of the aircraft by RAF parachute jump instructors (PJI) who stay in the plane after we have left. With the German Military you are dispatched by a jump instructor from your own unit who then follows the last man out.

During my German Para course I was dispatched and followed by the commandant of the Parachute Training School. He was a fantastic man who had more jumps logged than most British units in total. He told me that no aircraft or helicopter ever took off with students on board unless he was with them. On one of my training jumps the colonel was to follow me out using a free-fall parachute and I had cleared it with him to exit looking backwards so that I could watch him.[59] I exited the plane at the normal German jump height of 1500 feet and was fascinated to see him dive out head first just behind me. As my 'chute deployed I watched as he pulled the ripcord only for his main parachute to malfunction, as he plummeted towards the ground he just managed to deploy his reserve before landing. When I landed I ran across the DZ to where the colonel had landed only to see him calmly packing his equipment away with a cigarette in his mouth and wondering what all the fuss was about.

On our return to the UK from this training exercise we were to parachute into a small DZ just outside Aldershot. Families and girl-friends were transported out to the area and a barbecue and bar were laid on. The parachuting went well but the presence of HM Customs officers on the DZ, to check our duty-free allowances, did deflate the affair slightly.

Airport or Bust

One overseas exercise saw us in a part of the United Arab Emirates, where we had to complete a tactical march from a beach landing, over mountains and across the desert to the country's international airport. Resting up during the heat of midday, we marched during the night and cool of the morning. Even so it took us five days, during which we were constantly resupplied by helicopter with water, to ease the dehydration, heat exhaustion and heat-stroke that took its toll on us. We were fully operationally kitted out for this, as we were supposedly a liberating force advancing across enemy occupied territory.

On the evening of the fourth day of this gruelling march, with blistered feet, aching backs and morale slipping, we were attacked by a small formation from the local defence force, which was acting as the enemy. They did, however, beat a rather hasty retreat when, disregarding the blank ammunition that they were firing at us, we fixed bayonets and charged their positions. This rather ancient form of military manoeuvre probably took into account that during the march most, if not all, of us had thrown away a fair quantity of our ammo in an attempt to reduce excess weight.

When we finally arrived at our objective, the base of the airfield water tower, we were reduced to forty per cent of our initial force.

Sky's the Limit, or is it?

As part of a unit exercise in Sudan, I was asked to assist with the free-fall training of a select group of Sudanese Officers and SNCOs, based in a barracks close to the centre of Khartoum. From there, each day, we would drive to a military airbase and go off free-falling, on to a DZ located at the junction of the Blue and White Nile rivers.

Because Sudan had changed military allegiance so often, this whole tasking was fraught with incidents, not helped by the fact that we were jumping out of Russian helicopters flown by Chinese-trained Arabs. At the start of one jump the main rotor gave off just as we took off. Mind you these were the only choppers I had flown in that had to travel down a runway to get up enough speed to take off. On another occasion we were out over the desert when a forty-gallon container, which was tied to some of the seats, tipped over and spilt aviation fuel all over the floor of the helicopter. Fortunately we had already dispatched our students, so it was a unanimous decision that we would be safer outside the helicopter than in, we just dived out and left the crew to sort their problem out.

As it was so hot during the day we would only parachute early each morning and later in the afternoon. This is because the helicopters could not climb to altitude in the thinner hot air. One afternoon we returned to the airfield to do some free-fall jumps without our students. Using the same airframe as the morning, but with a crew we had not met before, our officer went off to brief the pilot on our planned descent. However, this ran into problems when the pilot refused to go to our required dropping height.

After discussing the weather forecast and the number of parachutists to be carried, our team leader demanded 'One pass over the release point at thirteen thousand.'

'Not possible,' stated the pilot, 'we can't get to that altitude with this helicopter.'

'It did this morning so why can't it this afternoon? It's cooler and there's less of a head wind', our leader inquired.

Flying hours were rare in the Sudanese Armed Forces at this time, due to financial restriction, and as the UK Government had donated the fuel for this training, our previous air crews had been very helpful and were more than willing to fly any routines we asked for.

'Thirteen thousand. Not possible', answered the pilot.

'Look, I want one pass at thirteen thousand feet and that's final', shouted our officer, slowly losing his patience with the pilot, whom he saw as a rather disagreeable and obnoxious man.

'Thirteen thousand feet?' inquired the pilot, 'that's different.'

'Why?' asked our team leader, 'what's different with that now and two minutes ago?'

'Well. We use metres and not feet and there is one big difference in thirteen thousand feet and thirteen thousand metres', replied the pilot.

Our intrepid leader walked off muttering things about 'bloody smarty pants pilots' and how, given one more flash comment, he would rip the man's head off and stuff it somewhere where the sun doesn't shine.

R &R in Sudan

During our time in Sudan, we used one of the only two legitimate places you could then get alcoholic beverages. This was a sumptuous relic from the days of the Empire, with large ceiling fans, marble floors and waiters in stiff white jackets. Just across the swimming pool from the bar was a lavish games room with two snooker tables. It was to this room that I was called one evening, when one of our officers had the misfortune to dislocate his shoulder while reaching across the table to take a shot. The poor chap had a history of his shoulder popping out following a parachuting accident a few years previously.

When I got into the games room he was sprawled over the table and in some pain. After slowly lifting him off and into a chair we placed one of the snooker balls in his armpit and quickly pulled and rotated his arm until the shoulder jumped back into place. We then retired to the bar to discuss our medical treatment.

On another day at this gin palace some of the lads were persuaded to part with a reasonable sum of money for a trip to see the battlefields of Omdurman. We were conveyed out into the desert in a small non-air-conditioned minibus and after an hour's ride were shown a strip of desert and told the history of the famous battle where Lord Kitchener defeated the Dervishes in 1898.

Unfortunately, there were no signs, plaques or memorials to convince us that we were at the actual battle site. It could have been any old strip of desert. Our guide could do nothing to convince us otherwise, so it was a group of rather cheesed-off teddies that returned to the club to drown their sorrows.

Quick Para Course

While on one of my jaunts abroad, the small unit I was with shared the camp with a battalion from one of the British Army's elite infantry regiments. They had funny ranks like Drill Sergeant, who was actually a Warrant Officer, which led initially to some confusion among us regular Army types. Nevertheless, we were soon enjoying each other's war stories in the Sergeants' Mess bar.

The SNCOs from the infantry would attempt to teach us some of the more intricate drill manoeuvres for which they were rightfully world famous and we would instruct them in the finer art of military parachuting. At the end of one long and arduous drinking session we decided that it was time for our students to go through an actual parachute descent and, if carried out correctly, they would be presented with their well-earned Parachute wings. The bar was cleared of glasses and bottles and one by one they climbed aboard. Following our instructions they had to correctly stand up, check equipment and face the door (the end of the bar). On our orders that the red light had come on, they were required to shuffle towards the door and on the green light exit the (very low flying) aircraft in the approved fashion. On hitting the floor, they had to carry out the correct actions to any one of the emergency drills we had taught them and finally execute an immaculate parachute landing and fall. If they did all this to our satisfaction they were deemed to have passed our crash course (sic) in military parachuting and were entitled to our version of the British Parachute badge.

Once they had all performed their test jump, the successful pupils formed up in front of the bar and were congratulated with a hearty handshake, a pint of beer and finally the coveted parachute badges were pinned onto their chests. Unfortunately for them we did not have any pins, so we fastened the 'wings' using an office staple gun . . .

Snakes Alive

It's always a shame to waste a good opportunity, or so my mate thought as he sweltered under the East African sun. Just prior to departing for this trip he had had a major falling out with the unit RSM and spent much of his time mulling over ways to get his own back on the man.

My mate spent a lot of his spare time wandering around the desert trying to find small snakes, spiders and scorpions. If he couldn't find any he would pay the locals to catch them for him. Anything venomous was a prize catch.

Once caught he would pack the creatures into individual jiffy bags and post them back to the RSM, who was back in the UK. It was my friend's dearest wish that at least one would survive the journey and when the package was opened, that it would bite his enemy, perhaps with fatal consequences.

Unfortunately, or fortunately depending which way you look at it, the RSM got suspicious of all the packages arriving in spite of the fact that when they were finally opened none of the contents were alive.

Half My Dog

One Friday afternoon those members of my new Special Forces regiment that were left in barracks with nothing else to do retired to one of the local watering holes. Our company was graced by one of the legends of the regiment, who had earned a fearsome reputation as a covert operator in Derry during the peak of the Northern Ireland Troubles working undercover disguised as a milkman.

Dandy was a tough campaign-hardened soldier who enjoyed nothing better than a few bottles of Guinness every so often. His usual practice was to buy a crate of twenty-four bottles and stand at the bar with his foot on them, while chatting to his comrades-in-arms.

This particular afternoon session came to a halt when Dandy's Irish wife burst into the bar. Screaming blue murder and using words that most of us had not heard before or understood, she set about her husband for failing to take her shopping as promised.

After many threats of physical abuse she stormed towards the door ranting about divorcing Dandy and taking half the family wealth back to southern Ireland. Just then Dandy spoke:

'Well, if that's the case. You can have half of these here empties, half my dog, and tomorrow morning you can have half my hangover.'

He then quietly returned to the task in hand and finished the crate of Guinness.

Saluting Problems

As is the norm in army units, notices of events and visits are published on Daily Unit Part One Orders.

Thus, one day we read that a really high-ranking VIP was to visit the Lines and that all personnel were reminded of the need to salute officers.[60] This regulation was normally not enforced in this particular

91

unit as it could lead to mistakes in the field and inadvertently identify an officer to the enemy.

One of the many unit characters still in the regiment at this time decided that, as the adjutant had issued this notice, he should be made to suffer the consequences.

So next morning as the adjutant parked his car in the HQ car park he was surprised to find a sergeant standing to attention by the car saluting. Then, as he reached the front door of the HQ building, the same sergeant was holding the door open for him while saluting.

After he had spoken to a few of the HQ personnel, the adjutant finally got to his second-floor office only to find the same SNCO standing in the corridor-saluting. Using a few well-chosen expletives, the officer told the sergeant to go away and stop hassling him. He then settled into his normal morning routine but was interrupted by a phone call that started, 'Sir, I'm saluting you now, sir'. He was interrupted again by a knock on his office window. Looking round he saw the same SNCO standing on a ladder outside his office and saluting.

That afternoon's Unit Daily Part One Orders stated that only officers of other units or foreign Armed Forces were, in future, to be saluted.

HRH His, HRH Hers

It used to be a regular thing for members of royalty, both from the UK and abroad, to visit one unit I worked with. On this occasion a husband and wife team arrived for a day of spills and thrills. As part of the itinerary they were to see an anti-terrorist exercise based on an embassy siege. Both of the VVIPs agreed to take part and were dressed in black flameproof overalls. He had 'HRH His' emblazoned on his and she had 'HRH Hers'.

As HRH His had been through this exercise several times before, HRH Hers was to take a more active roll. First, they were to watch a complete demonstration, then take part in a second similar exercise. Both HRHs stood to one side as the siege began and watched as a helicopter hovered overhead and abseil ropes were lowered. Four bodies could be seen getting out of the helicopter as it hovered at a hundred feet above the embassy roof. As they began their descent, one appeared to lose his grip and plunged head first onto the roof with a sickening thud. HRHs looked on with shock but stood in open-mouthed amazement when the man reappeared over the parapet of the roof, brushed himself down and continued with the assault. (A fully-equipped dummy had deliberately been allowed to fall and the man had been hidden on the roof before the demonstration started.)

Next came their chance to show what they were made of. HRH His joined a team that entered the embassy via the front door and HRH Hers joined an assault team that were to go in through an upstairs window.

HRH Hers insisted on driving the assault team's Range Rover, which she did with such skill that some of the team jumped off just before she executed a perfect handbrake turn and stopped one foot from the embassy wall. One of the team had been told to follow HRH Hers and make sure she came to no harm, which was fortunate as she nearly did.

Standing at the bottom of the assault ladder, she watched as the rest of the team climbed up and through the window. At the same time stun grenades were being fired through adjacent windows and one missed, hit the wall and dropped next to HRH Hers. As this exploded and jumped around a spark flew off and hit HRH Hers, setting the lacquer on her beautifully coiffeured hair alight. Her minder quickly patted out the flames and pushed HRH Hers up the ladder in an attempt to take her mind off it.

At the end of the assault HRH Hers was asked if she had enjoyed herself.'Oh yes. Most certainly; it was rather thrilling. But why did someone keep hitting me around the head just before I went up the ladder?'

Jungle Stories

One of the great factors of life in the Special Forces is your ability to survive in any environment; thus we often went off to places far across the seas to practise these skills and learn new techniques. It was on one of these trips to the jungles of the Far East that I had the pleasure of observing a soldier who was not really cut out for this type of work and was in fact physically and mentally traumatised by the thought of such nasties as snakes, spiders and blood-sucking leeches.

After a long hard morning's navigation training around our local area we were allowed to collapse, tactically of course, at the edge of a track and make a quick brew of tea. While making my cuppa I also kept an eye out for my colleague who genuinely thought that the whole jungle would either bite you, give you a nasty rash or simply kill you.

There he was, bergen still on his back, as he cleared a small patch of jungle floor with his machete. He then took off his bergen and proceeded to sit on it. It was as he did this that he was mortified to see a small leech disappearing through the leather of his left boot. Letting out a blood-chilling scream he picked up his machete and took a full-arm swing at the offending leech. Unfortunately for this man, he was somewhat over vigorous in his actions and managed to split the boot into two, and yes, his foot didn't fair much better. The medic had to spend much time and effort in stemming the flow of blood while the squad instructor called in a helicopter to medivac the now hobbling soldier out of this most feared environment.

On the same trip we had to medivac another soldier who had inadvertently not paid much attention to the lecture on the multi-usage of the common condom. As any old soldier will tell you, you not only use this item while satisfying your sexual needs. In the jungle you can use it to carry water and, by placing it over the end of the barrel of your rifle, you stop dirt from getting down the barrel without having to remove it should you need to fire the weapon.

One of the other uses for condoms in the jungle is to stop leeches attaching themselves to your penis. Jungle-savvy soldiers wear condoms whenever there is a chance of this happening and this is increased should you have to do river crossing or are in really damp swampy areas. It was in this area that the unfortunate soldier learnt his lesson, when a large bull leech not only attached itself to his manhood but also somehow managed to get into his urethra, where it started to engorge itself on his blood. Severe pain soon followed and even after the maximum dose of morphine had been administered, the poor man was in great difficulty. Yet another helicopter was called in and the chap eventually went under the surgeon's knife to remove the poor leech.

Follow the Officer

I was deployed to a small camp in Central America where the British Army used to keep a battalion group in case the country next door carried out its threat to invade. I was the sole representative of my organisation at this location and used to spend most of my time wandering around the villages carrying out Hearts and Minds visits.[61] I reported back to my base, which was at the other end of the country, once a week and tried to have nothing much to do with my host unit. They did not like me much as I did not wear clean pressed uniforms, had my hair slightly longer than they allowed and carried the much lighter American Armalite rifle against their heavy FN Self-Loading Rifle or SLR.

With consent from my commander I was asked to accompany a foot patrol into an area that this unit had not been to before. The briefing was held the day before and during this I was introduced to the officer and SNCO who would lead the patrol. Unfortunately the officer was a fresh-faced second lieutenant, who took great exception to me being tagged on to his patrol and he made this quite plain when we talked at the end of the formal briefing.[62]

'Now listen here,' started the lieutenant, 'I'm in charge of this patrol. I want you to stay at the back with my sergeant and only interfere if I ask for your help. Do you understand?'

'Very clear, sir. My brief is to assist you if you require it but also to make certain that nothing nasty happens, and that we all get back here in one piece.'

'I do not want you making me look incompetent in front of my men. Understood?'

'A hundred per cent clear, sir. It's your patrol', I said as I went off to check my kit ready for an early morning start.

Next day at 0730 hours I went down to the heli-pad ready to meet the troops and deploy by Puma helicopter into the patrol area. The first thing that struck me was the rucksacks the lads were carrying. They appeared far too heavy for a three-day patrol, so I asked one of the soldiers what he had inside his. Ten days of ammunition, ten days of water and ten days of rations. The rations were in their issued boxes and could not be opened unless needed.[63] All as per the lieutenant's orders.

The helicopters finally arrived and the twenty-one of us emplaned as per the briefing. I went with the officer in the first Puma and the sergeant was in charge of the second group. Ten or fifteen minutes later we landed at the HLZ (helicopter landing zone), with rotors still turning, we jumped out of the helicopters and went into a defensive posture to secure the HLZ. From who or what I was not sure but that was what the officer wanted.

Once both groups were safely on the ground the lieutenant stood in the middle of the HLZ, consulted map and compass and headed off into the jungle. As briefed, the patrol fell in behind him and I took up my designated position at the rear. The officer set off at a cracking pace and some of the patrol found it hard going with all their kit. Many had not been in the country long and were not properly acclimatised.

After an hour's hard march the officer called a tea-break and the lads fell off the track and lay sweating and too knackered to make a brew. I took the opportunity to walk along the patrol with their sergeant, checking that all was well. When we reached the front I asked the lieutenant if all was OK and if he had any problems.

'No', he barked ungraciously. 'No problems at all and I told you to stay at the rear of this patrol.'

'I fully understand, sir. But could you give me a six-figure grid reference of where you think we are.'

'What! You are supposed to be the local expert and how dare you question my ability. Of course I know where we are', he howled. After much muttering and studying of his map he gave me the answer.

'Sorry, sir. Just wanted to check', I said as I headed back to make a quick mug of tea.

Tea break over, we resumed our tramp through the jungle. Sticking to well-defined paths we could move fairly quickly, even allowing for the totally unnecessary weight that the patrol was carrying. Just after midday our leader called for another stop and lunch break for forty-five minutes. Again the sergeant and I walked along checking the patrol. Some of the lads had blisters forming on their feet and areas of erosion on their backs and waists caused by heavy sweating and chaffing of their equipment.

Reaching the front I again asked the lieutenant if all was well.

'You are beginning to annoy me', he started. 'You were told to stay at the rear and not to interfere unless I requested it. Is that understood?'

'Absolutely, sir. But may I have your permission to set up my radio and could you give me an eight-figure grid reference this time for our current position.'

Looking more than a touch impatient and slightly harassed, he found his map, which was lying on the ground next to his rifle, and reeled off eight numbers.

'Why do you want a grid reference again and why set up your radio? You don't have a scheduled call until 1800 hours', he asked.

'Sir, with all due respect, I really should contact my commander and let him know what is going on here.' The officer looked at me not too sure of what I meant. 'I think he will agree that we need to call back the helicopter and get out of this area.'

'What?' he bellowed. 'Why on earth would we need to do that? I'm in charge here and I demand that you do no such thing.'

'Sir. We are ten kilometres over the border at present. In effect, sir, we are in enemy territory. You obviously do not know where we are and I want us out of here before nightfall.'

After much wrangling over the radio net, we were told to head back to the border as fast as we could go, dumping rations and water if necessary. Once we were on safe soil two Puma helicopters picked us up. Back at base all hell let loose and our trusty young leader tried to lay the blame on anyone but himself. He even tried to talk his way out of the mess by explaining that his map did not match the ground and that his compass didn't work correctly. With the backing of the patrol's sergeant, I was able to tell the true side of the story and our leader was severely reprimanded.

It is perhaps true that the deadliest thing in the world is a British Army officer with a map and compass.

Canadian Parachute Training

At the end of a training exercise in Canada we were given the chance to do some parachute jumps with their airborne forces and gain our

Canadian wings. Only two of us volunteered, my partner was an RAF PJI who had completed many hundreds of jumps, not only military static-line but free-fall as well. He had been a member of the RAF parachute display team for many years and was a military free-fall instructor to boot.

The Canadian students we joined were fascinated that we should enjoy parachuting so much that we had given up part of our end-of-exercise holiday to do this. They were also amazed at the actual number of parachute jumps we each had. They logged all parachute activity, even the jumps that were cancelled, for whatever reason, were recorded by them as Stop Drops. Unlike us Brits, who received a small daily bonus for Parachute pay, the Canadians were paid for each jump completed.

Two things stick in my mind about this training. One was that every instruction given by Canadians had to be given in English and French. This made the shortest announcement or order into a major speech. In the British Airborne you went and drew your Para equipment from a store or van and individually adjusted the harness to fit yourself. The Canadians were verbally guided through each step at a time, in French and English. To get a first-light descent meant that you had to start at midnight.

The second thing I remember was on one of the training jumps we were to do from a helicopter. My partner and I were teamed up with four Canadian officers, to make a team of six parachutists for the heli-lift. It was only as we sat in the helicopter, three each side, that we noticed that the four officers with us were all military chaplains. Were our hosts trying to tell us something?

What a Lucky Chap

A warm sunny summer's day saw ten of us aboard an RAF Hercules C130 transport plane circling a parachute DZ in the Midlands. We had managed to bum a lift on a Basic Parachute Training Course flight and were due to jump out after the students had been dispatched.[64] In those days training jumps were done from 800 feet and in various configurations of groups. Single sticks (or chalks) from one side door at a time, simultaneous sticks from both sides, and with increasing stick sizes until the whole aircraft emptied in one pass over the DZ.

The trainee Paras were to do a Sim Stick jump of fifteen paratroopers from each side door (known as a Sim 15) and we stood up at the back of the aircraft on the tailgate watching as the obviously nervous students went through their drills and prepared to exit. We all knew what they were going through as we had been there at some stage in our military careers but sympathy was not on the programme this day; their faces went from pale pink to white to plain old ashen as the drop time neared.

When the red light came on the students were at action stations, lead man in the open door facing out into the clear blue sky and the force of the back blast as the plane thundered through the sky. As the warning lights changed to green, the sticks disappeared out through the doors at the usual fast pace that only the British Airborne could manage.[65] As they did this one of my comrades leapt across the plane and seemed to grab the last man on the port side stick before pushing him out into space. With the aircraft empty apart from us and the three RAF Parachute Jump Instructors (RAF PJI), we all wanted to know what the hell our friend had done to the poor student, it had happened so quickly that only the men involved had any idea what had taken place.[66]

It transpired that the last man in the stick had performed one of his pre-jump drills incorrectly and had ended up with the static line, which would automatically deploy his parachute, wrapped round his neck. Had he, in fact, exited the aircraft like this, the combined forces of his body weight, the effects of the slipstream and forward motion of the plane would undoubtedly have ripped his head off.

When we had completed our own training jump we met up with the trainees and tracked down the soldier who had been the last man in the port stick. The only thing he could recall was having a very rough ride down the slipstream, which he put down to hitting the side of the door as he exited. He went a very funny shade of pale when we enlightened him. The RAF PJI who should have checked him prior to dispatching him was hauled over the coals for this but in the end it just comes down to the fact that that trainee Para was a very lucky chap.

Wild African Safaris

On one of my trips to Kenya we had a scout helicopter team attached to us. The pilots were commercial pilots who, as members of the TA, were completing their annual camp. The helicopters were primarily used to support our field firing, navigation, and tactical training but could be used for other missions if they could be justified.

One day the helicopter was not tasked with anything military, so we hopped aboard and went on an airborne safari. It was fantastic to swoop down over herds of elephant, giraffe, gazelle and the odd lion. The good thing about being in a helicopter was that if we saw something really interesting we could simply hover above it and take as many photographs as we wanted.

We also used the choppers for the odd spot of free-fall parachuting but the pilots were nervous about flying at any great height as the dropping zone was in fact several hundred feet above sea level and the air was extremely thin even on the ground, let alone at altitude.

One of the pilots, in particular, could be a pain while flying us and would have to be repeatedly asked to correct his run-in and flight pattern to get us to our desired release point. So a plan was hatched to finally make or break him. My friend and I would be the last two to leave the chopper and I would direct the drop. After dispatching two other free-fallers I asked the pilot to go around again and to gain height. He was very reluctant to do this but finally swung the helicopter into a circular ascent and I directed him on to our release point.

Just as we approached the spot where we would exit, my friend and I climbed out of either side of the chopper and made our way forward along the helicopter's skids. Much to the horror of the pilot we then proceeded to clean the windscreen, before executing back-flips away from the chopper. I think this was the first time the pilot had ever actually seen anyone outside a plane at altitude and when he landed he was in a state of shock.

Jungle Stories

The jungle was my favourite training area and I visited Brunei on numerous occasions. The country as a whole was fascinating, the people friendly and the jungle a challenge.

After one particularly hard day lugging our resupply from the nearest HLZ we sat down to a nice cup of tea and, with mouths watering, watched as our fresh rations cooked.[67] Jacko, Chalky and I had been on this task for six weeks now and apart from smelling like the jungle and not washing or shaving for the whole time, our clothes were beginning to rot from the constant damp and effects of our sweat. So any little treat was fondly anticipated.

Jacko was lying on his pole bed under his mosquito net, as Chalky and I sat a few feet away supervising the cooking.[68] All of a sudden there was the loud creaking sound of wood bending, followed by a very loud snap. All three of us knew that this was the unmistakable noise of a 'dead fall'. This is when the top branches of a tree die and fall off. These can be just a few feet of wood or a few tonnes of lumber.

We also knew by the sound that the dead fall was directly above us. Chalky and I jumped up and ran away from the anticipated danger area. Jacko also tried to leave but for some reason got caught up in his mosquito net and was still fighting his way out when the branches hit the ground just to one side of his pole bed. Had he not been caught up he probably would have been hit by the falling braches and seriously, if not fatally, injured.

One other thing ruined our day. The branches had landed on our cooker and completely decimated our fresh rations.

On another trip into the Brunei jungle, we were all sleeping soundly after a day's jungle tactic training when I suddenly felt something crawling across my forehead. Accepting that it was a small insect I swatted it and tried to go back to sleep. Only to be annoyed again by something else moving across my face. Breaking all the laws of jungle warfare, I decided to use my pocket torch and see what the problem was.

To my utter amazement I looked up to see the inside of my basha (military jargon for field sleeping area/tent/bivouac) covered in ants. Jumping out of bed and from under my mosquito net I stood and beat the insects from my clothing.[69] Having woken some of the others they got up to see what all the fuss was about. We found out that a colony of wood ants had decided to move house from one tree to another and my basha just happened to be in the way. It took two and a half hours for them to move home, before I could return to my bed and try to catch up on some much needed sleep.

Sorry We're Late

After one jungle trip, five of us decided to spend our R & R in one of the neighbouring countries.[70] We flew directly into the country and were booked into a good quality hotel. Our seven days would be spent touring the capital city and relaxing in some of the local hostelries, discos and casinos.

The hotel had a nice open-air bar on the roof and some of the lads would head up there for a nightcap. One thing that caught your eye from this vantage point was that just across the road was the embassy of one of the world superpowers and we knew that the grounds would be fully monitored and perhaps even criss-crossed by pressure-sensitive pads and/or infra-red beams to alert the embassy guards to intruders. So some of my chums would spend an hour or two, late at night, hurling empty beer bottles into the embassy compound and then watching the guards rush around looking for the intruder, or even a saboteur or spy.

Every day throughout our R & R we went to a twenty-four hour open-air disco that was just around the corner from the hotel. There we became very friendly with the resident female singing group, who would join us at our table for drinks in between their sessions. We even joined them on stage as their dance troupe and generally had a great time.

However, just after our arrival at the disco, on the first night, one of our group went into the gents' toilet and had a nasty experience. Standing at the urinal he was stunned and amazed when someone came up behind him and started to massage his shoulders. His first reaction was to spin round and thump the weirdo on the jaw. It turned out that it was normal practice for the toilet attendant to do this, and he also provided hot towels and cologne for customers after they had washed their hands. Unfortunately no one had told us this and the outcome was that the young chap had to take a few hours off to get his swollen jaw attended to.

On the last day of our R & R we sent our bags to the airport and we went to the open-air disco to say goodbye to the girls. It was our plan to have a few drinks and then travel on to the airport for our flight to Hong Kong. Needless to say we overstayed our time at the disco and were rather drunk when we tried to book in for the flight. The airline staff refused point blank to allow us to join the flight even after we explained that we had a connecting Royal Air Force flight out of Hong Kong to London the same day.

What could we do? We were broke and booked out of our hotel and had nowhere to stay. Plus we had to inform our unit that we would not be able to join them on their flight to the UK. After some alcoholically induced quick thinking we decided our best plan of action was to call the military attaché at the British embassy. After much hassle we managed to get through to his office and explain our plight. We were told to wait where we were and they would arrange something.

To our amazement a Royal Naval Commander arrived, in full tropical rig, straight from some embassy party. He was none too pleased when he saw us but told us that he had arranged for us to return to our hotel and that we had to go to the embassy the next morning as they would re-book our flights. We explained that we had no money left, so he very likely lent us some. He then stormed off back to his party and we went back to the disco.

Next morning we jumped into a taxi and headed for the British embassy. Notwithstanding that the taxi driver did not know where the embassy was and we had to stop and ask a friendly policeman, we finally arrived at the military attaché's office. They informed us that they had contacted our unit and that they had arranged civilian flights for us back to London, via Singapore, that afternoon. We had some forms to fill in and then went directly to the airport.

After a very social overnight stop in Singapore, namely at the bars along the infamous Buggies Street, we arrived in London and went straight to our unit. On reporting to the RSM, we were informed that no action would be taken for our absence until a full report arrived from the British embassy. We were allowed to go on three weeks' leave and when we reported back were told that as we had to pay for the extra night at the hotel (at full rates) and the civilian flights, plus repay the money lent by the naval commander, the CO thought that pun-

ishment enough. Our individual pay accounts were debited for
£1,846.50.

Drink and Drink Some More

As you may have noted from earlier passages in this book, drink
played a major part in the life of the average soldier. This seemed to
be even more so in the Airborne and SF units that I worked with. Not
that I'm making any form of critical comment, I would be the last to
leave any bar if there was still beer available.

Even so, some of my fellow military dipsomaniacs were quite out-
standing. One that instantly comes to mind was a SF chap who would
gamble as to how many times he could walk around his crowded local
pub with a full pint of beer balanced on his head. This trick would be
performed late into the night and usually when he was well over the
recommended driving limit.

James would do his party piece two or three times a night, every
night. He would then be seen trying to dance in the city's discos until
the wee hours of the morning. Nevertheless the most amazing thing
would greet you as you staggered into barracks the next morning and
that would be the sight of James setting off for his daily run. Whether
this was to keep fit or to run off some of the alcohol I was never sure,
but it seemed to work for him.

Camp Alarms

Part of the introduction for a selection course I used to work on
included a briefing by the company sergeant major on security and
camp alarms. He did the same speech at least twice a year and it
always drew a similar response.

'Right. The alarm for a fire in the camp is a siren sounding for thirty
seconds, thirty seconds off, then thirty seconds on again. This will
continue until I tell the guard to shut it off.'

He continued, 'The alarm for a camp attack is a siren sounding for
thirty seconds, thirty seconds off, then thirty seconds on again. This
will continue until I tell the guard to shut it off. Any questions.'

There was always one brave student who would ask 'But, sergeant major, how will we know if it's a fire or camp attack?'

'Well, laddie,' the CSM would say, 'in a camp attack you get the sound of musketry in the background.'

De-identify Yourself

Also as part of the the selection course, which was to find suitable personnel from all three services (male and female) for duties as covert intelligence operators, students had to 'de-identify' themselves. They were told not to discuss their backgrounds with each other, to remove all items or labels that could indicate their parent arm/service, rank or name. This was done as soon as the students arrived at the camp and they were warned that checks on their efficiency to adhere to this order would be carried out. Each student was given a number and name, i.e. George, Jill, Bill or other such handle.

So, as forewarned, at 0400 hours the next morning all the instructors would muster outside the students' accommodation and the fire alarm would sound. As soon as this happened we would rush into the accommodation blocks and tell the students to parade outside immediately; they were allowed no time to dress or linger in their barrack rooms. Once all of them were outside we would go to a barrack room and await their return.

After a slow roll-call, the students would be herded back into the barracks and told to stand next to their beds.[71] The only segregation allowed was that females occupied separate barrack blocks; otherwise all ranks and services were mixed in together. The instructors would then split into pairs and work their way through the rooms checking every student thoroughly. It did not matter how well they had hidden things we had all the time in the world to find stuff and did we find it.

I remember opening someone's wash bag to find a Post Office savings book in there. The student stated that he had kept it just in case he needed any money. One student I searched had a furry fox at the top of his bed with his pyjamas inside, unfortunately I also found a set of epaulettes with his unit title and rank on them. Another student had his chequebook, credit card and driving licence hidden in a rolled-up pair of socks. The list went on and on, and the students soon learnt that NAAFI labels and service laundry labels could actually identify someone.

Loud Mouth

One item on the selection courses for a particular unit required students to run round an indoor assault course continuously for one hour. The Physical Training Instructors (PTIs) would chase them up and note any weak or injured students. They would also look out for anyone pacing himself or herself, or holding back at a certain obstacle. As the students had to display their course number on their chests and trouser legs it was easy to note any individual. During this session the course would be halted from time to time and one of the PTIs would be introduced to them. On this particular course I was known as PT 2 and the others by similar tags.

At the end of the session the students were moved straight into a large lecture theatre and told to sit down. Still sweating and out of breath they would be instructed to write physical descriptions of certain members of the PT staff. Those members would obviously not be in the room at this point.

After thirty minutes the students were told to stop and to ensure that they had written their course number on the top of each page completed. Those PTIs whose descriptions were required then came back into the class so that the students could check their answers. While they did this we would walk around looking at their work. I was most impressed by one student's description of PT 4, a female instructor who specialised in unarmed combat.

I called PT 4 over so that she could review this particular student's description of herself and was not too surprised when she knocked the student to the floor with a well-aimed right hook. He had described PT 4 as five foot ten inches tall, white with dark brown hair and as being a 'loud-mouthed lesbian'. Needless to say this man had a very hard time for the rest of his stay and withdrew voluntarily from the course after ten days.

Chariot Race

Towards the end of one selection course we would send the students out for a two-day, three-night exercise. This entailed them splitting into groups of two or three and manning a small observation point. We would then send cars, joggers and walkers past all the locations so that the students could practise their observation skills by logging the events. We did not give them much equipment so they had to make the best of their surroundings. We did not feed or water them too often either.

The exercise would end an hour or so before dawn, when we would visit all the teams and tell them to pack up quickly and move to a rendezvous point. Once there we checked that all were present and then moved them off about three hundred yards at the double. One of the instructors would make a fuss about the students being hungry so we would stop them and ask if this was true. They of course would answer yes and much to their amazement a truck would appear and we would unload some food containers. However, the only food available was some very salty porridge. With the students lined up along each side of the road, we would ensure that they each had a very large helping. Then it was off again, at the double, across the training area. The next halt was about two kilometres from the camp, where we would prepare them for the next surprise.

Prepositioned at this spot would be three Land Rover three-quarter ton vehicles, each with two tow-ropes attached to the front bumper. Quickly splitting the students into three teams, the task would be described to them. It was very simple; they had to race back to camp with each team pulling a Land Rover. Anyone failing to stay with their 'chariot' would be classed as a failure and RTUd from the course.[72]

As we set off one of the instructors would be in the driver's seat of each vehicle to assist with the steering. However, on this particular morning it was raining heavily and the sky was still very dark. The tracks and roads we used for this were not particularly wide so we, the instructors, had to watch for student safety whenever a team passed another. With everybody screaming and shouting it could get a bit hectic. If a team looked as if they were pulling away too easily or not working too well, the instructor in the driver's seat would apply a little pressure on the brake pedal.

Halfway through the driver of the last vehicle thought he had hit a pothole, or some such thing, and looked in his rearview mirror only to see a student lying in the road. As we always had medical back-up they were able to attend to the student and the race continued uninterrupted.

It turned out that the student was from the third chariot team and had fallen under the vehicle. Luckily for him (and us) he had fallen on a very soft part of the track and as the Land Rover ran over his leg it had buried it in the mud. His only injuries were a few minor abrasions and a bruise, but this did mean that he got RTUd.

Who's Listening to Me?

During one part of the training for a covert unit I would act as the known baddie and lead the students off across the UK to a small city on the west coast. The students would have to put into practice all the skills they had been taught so far. This included surveillance (on foot, by vehicle or in static posts), photography, radio procedures, search techniques and fast driving.

I would book into a small hotel and then roam around the city meeting contacts and doing other suspicious activities. This would be done in my car, on foot, by public transport and even on a hired bicycle. All the time the students had to record my activities and report them back to the instructors. If the surveillance became too obvious I would increase the degree of difficulty for the followers, to the extent that I would perhaps book into a gymnasium and then sit in the sauna for a few hours.

While I was out of my hotel room the students would have to break into the room and search it. All without leaving a trace and, more importantly, without letting the hotel staff know what was going on. Fortunately, all the times that I did this exercise no one was ever caught.

One favourite trick was to lead all the follow-up cars to a small toll bridge over a large gorge just outside the city. Crossing the bridge was controlled by traffic signals and only one direction could travel over the bridge at a time. Fortunately for me but not for the students this was a very busy area and it was impossible to get to the other side of the gorge without a lengthy detour. I would wait until all the following cars were queued up behind me to cross the bridge and then drive over, execute a quick U-turn on the other side and join the queue to re-cross the bridge.

The look on their faces as they passed me and realised that they were now going in the wrong direction was always a delight.

The pièce de résistance for any student that got a little too cocky would be to get him, or her, to follow me into a coffee bar that I had used many times. Once the student(s) was in the café I would order a coffee and review the menu. Seeing this the students would have to order something to cover the anticipated time at their table and they would also have to use their covert radios to inform their controllers and other surveillance team members what was going on.

Two things would always happen at this point. First, the radio messages the students sent would be broadcast over the café's sound system.[73] The expression on their faces and reactions would be fantastic. Secondly, as soon as I noted the students receive their food order I would leave quickly and watch as they tried to follow.

Campaigns and Conflicts

The problems in Northern Ireland continued throughout my time in the Army. I participated in various capacities during the Dhofar, Falklands and Gulf Wars. I also acted as a union-breaking Blackleg when the military supported the civil populace during the national strikes of the fire and ambulance services, not to mention when we cleared rubbish from the streets of Glasgow during the dustmen's strike.

Letters From Home

Towards the end of one campaign, a senior officer with us wrote to his wife back in Scotland. He was so immensely proud of the letter that he allowed us to see part of it.

Dear Margaret

I have been here now for just over five months and have only three weeks to go. Even though life has been rough, certain temptations have been placed before me. However, my dearest, I can honestly say that I have remained faithful to our marriage vows.

Six months without you and the lack of our glorious sex life has left me drained. Therefore I plead with you, Margaret, to ensure that you meet me directly off the plane with a mattress strapped to your back and wearing nothing under your fur coat . . .

You never expect a senior officer to conduct himself in such a way, especially when you know that he has been seeing one of the expatriate wives from the construction company compound a mile away.

The reply was as good, if not better, and again the colonel allowed us to see it.

Dear Philip

Many thanks for your rather unusual letter. I too have remained totally faithful to our wedding vows and have had to beat off the milkman, butcher, gardener and postman.

Of course, my dearest, I will meet you at the bottom of the aircraft steps with a mattress tied to my back and be assured I will be desperate for sex as well.

However, Philip, you will have to make sure you are the first one off the plane.

Me RSM-You Officer

During deployment on one conflict, while I was talking to a Unit RSM who had been a friend for many years, I was amazed at a conversation he had with a very junior officer who meandered past.

Having reason to speak to the officer on a personal disciplinary matter (the appalling state of his dress and the length of his hair), the RSM used all due courtesy and respect to the officer. Nevertheless, the young subaltern took offence at being lectured at by the RSM and attempted to rebuke him for his insolence. Not one to raise his hackles easily or known for verbiage, the RSM allowed the subaltern to finish his diatribe and then recalled a short anecdote to conclude the conversation.

'Sir, when I joined the Army my greatest wish was to become a Regimental Sergeant Major, the highest non-commissioned rank attainable. And I presume, sir, that when you joined The Royal Military Academy, Sandhurst, your ultimate goal was to become a Field Marshal, as that is highest commissioned rank possible. Well, sir, I am an RSM and you are not a Field Marshal.'

The young officer thought about this for a second or two, blushed, apologised to the RSM and slouched off.

What an Eyesore

One unit that deployed during a recent campaign was located in a disused maternity hospital and had to erect a massive tented complex to accommodate its personnel, sub-unit departments and HQ. As this was a desert campaign, heat was a serious problem, made worse by the fact that inside the tented camp they had installed a series of protective liners, whose primary function was to safeguard the personnel should chemical or biological agents be used by the enemy. Unfortunately, these airtight enclosures served one other purpose and that was to make working or living inside them unbearable due to the heat. Various ideas were tried to reduce this problem but all to no avail.

None the less, the Unit Quartermaster finally came up with what he considered the perfect solution. That was to paint the outside of the tents to reflect rather than absorb the heat. With his commanding officer's approval, he purchased tins and tins of paint and set the unit personnel to work with brushes and rollers.

Unfortunately this did not reduce the inside temperature sufficiently but caused two new headaches for the unit. One was that the tents were now so coated in paint as to make the fabric too hard to take down and move. Thus a once highly mobile unit became a static facility. Secondly, and perhaps more importantly, pilots from a nearby airbase, started complaining that they were being blinded by reflected sunlight.

All caused by the liberal use of many gallons of metallic-based silver paint.

Doctors and Guns

Strolling around our desert camp one morning, I mentioned to the RSM a signal I (the unit's RQMS) had received. This was from a unit in our last location asking if I knew the whereabouts of a 9mm pistol that had going missing from their armoury. As we had stored our weapons in their armoury we could have inadvertently taken it as one of ours. I was a hundred per cent certain that we had not, but you never knew.

As we continued our daily stroll we noticed an officer walking in front of us with a shoulder holster and pistol. Both of us were convinced that this chap should not be in possession of such things-he was a reservist doctor called up to support the regulars during this conflict and I knew that he had not been issued with a one of our Browning pistols.[74]

The RSM confronted the officer about this and asked to see the weapon and we could not believe our luck when it miraculously turned out to be the one mentioned in the signal. The said officer was escorted in front of the adjutant where he was asked what the hell he was doing with it. He stated that as he was going to war and if current weapon scales did not allow him to be armed at all, he had decided to sign a weapon out from another unit's stock. A sentiment I had to agree with as I would not have wished to be sited close to the enemy border where I could be placed on a full war footing at any time, armed with only a Red Cross armband and a stethoscope.

However, the weapon had to be returned to its rightful owner, who was under threat of severe disciplinary action for losing it. The RSM explained to the officer that as he had taken the weapon illegally he should be responsible for its return.

That evening the RSM and I were called to the defence perimeter by one of the guard, who had seen someone standing by the perimeter and appearing to throw something out into the desert. The guard thought he could identify the person concerned. So as an immediate search of the area was carried out the guard was sent off to bring the suspect in front of the RSM. The search revealed a small quantity of unexpended 9mm ammunition.

As it turned out, the guard returned with none other than the officer involved with the missing pistol. Confronting the officer with the ammunition that had been recovered, the RSM asked him what he had been up to now. The officer told us that he had acted according to our instructions and returned the pistol to the correct armoury and was doing nothing more than just getting rid of the ammunition that he had no use for. For a second time that day the reservist medical officer stood in front of the unit adjutant and received a short, lucid but cogently constructed lecture on correct military procedures.

The next day a couple of Military Policemen arrived and wanted to see both the RSM and myself. It appeared that they had just been called to the Field Post Office to inspect a suspicious parcel, which had been sent from our unit lines. It turned out that our trusty officer had tried to return the pistol to the armoury concerned by sending it through the military postal system in a plain brown padded envelope.

Flowers in the Desert

As the threat of war increased, more and more units deployed into desert locations along the enemy's border. One such unit had a rather noxious officer in command, who had the man-management skills more akin to the Kray twins or Ghengis Khan than a British Army officer.

This officer insisted his RQMS build a small flower garden around the entrance to his command tent. 'Where would one get flowers, trellis, etc. in the desert, especially during a war?' asked the RQMS.

Unperturbed by this minor inconvenience the commanding officer sent the RQMS, a sergeant and a driver back to town to buy the required essential stores. This involved a ten-hour journey, one way and an overnight stop in town to accomplish the task. Unfortunately the first batch of flowers and shrubs perished and the whole thing had to be repeated.

As in any conflict, logistics are a major part of any battle plan and in a desert campaign the supply of potable water is always an important logistics problem. This particular unit had several hundred personnel on strength and they had to rely on road tankers getting to them with enough water for their daily needs. Sometimes the logistics chain would fail and not enough water would arrive. On one occasion when this happened the commanding officer made the decision to limit the amount of water for showers and washing. This meant that personnel were only able to wash once a day and shower twice a week. Not a pleasant thing to have to do but war is war. However, after several days of not being able to wash as and when necessary, some of the personnel took great exception to the fact that large quantities of the now precious water were being wasted each day. On the commanding officer's direct instructions, members of the guard had to water the flourishing command post garden twice a day and God help anyone that failed to adhere to this ludicrous order.

When confronted about this by one of his own senior officers, the commanding officer replied that it was 'his train set and he would play with it as he wanted'. This did not go down too well with one of the unit, who burst into the command post armed with his rifle and threatened to shoot the CO.

As the story of the incident leaked to higher formation headquarters, the NCO was transferred to another unit for the rest of the campaign but no further disciplinary action was taken against him.

As for the commanding officer, the last I heard of this raving demigod was when he tackled the MoD as to why he had not been put forward for an award or medal after the conflict.

Follow Me Troops

It is a sad fact of military life that logistics or support units are usually the last to leave any theatre of operations. At the end of one conflict some of these units had been deployed for over six months. So when orders for the demobilisation of one such unit were received, morale rose and smiles were seen on faces for the first time in ages.

To ensure that all necessary arrangements were going smoothly and according to plan, that accommodation, airplanes, road transport and meals were all in place for his unit, the commanding officer and one of his senior officers were the first unit personnel to return from the field to the base area.

Satisfied that all was correct, the officers sent a signal back to the unit explaining how the move would be conducted. Unfortunately for the rest of the unit the two officers had somehow managed to secure seats on a plane leaving for the UK that day. So by the time the signal was received and understood by the unit, its two illustrious leaders were already in the air and dreaming of home.

116

Tents for You-Hotel for Me

As the build-up to war gathered pace most of the units were deployed to their field locations. Battle preparation and practice continued as each unit readied itself for the thrust across the border into enemy territory.

Life under these circumstances is not pleasant and morale is hard to maintain. One way of achieving this is for the men to see that their officers are right with them and suffering as well. Not so with one particular unit.

As the men worked in blistering heat, broken only by the worst rainfalls in recorded history, with vehicles disappearing up to their wheel arches in rain-sodden soft sand and their tented accommodation beneath water on numerous occasions, morale was at its lowest.

This was further lowered when the commanding officer decided that as the war proper had not yet started there was no real need for him to stay in the field overnight with his unit. Responsibility would be passed to his second-in-command as each evening the CO drove off across the desert in his command vehicle, returning from his hotel room next morning.

Oh! What a Waste

As the inevitable war loomed, we watched all the satellite TV news programmes for information.[75] One of the UK channels showed its reporters dressed in full desert pattern camouflage uniform, desert boots and body armour.[76] This slightly miffed us as we were sitting ready for the ground war to kick off, had been in the country for several months and still had not been issued with any of the desert kit. We had to make do with uniforms designed for the European theatre or, if we were lucky enough, we could wear jungle uniform if we had it.

Finally, after many months in theatre, each member of the unit was measured for his/her desert uniform; we were to receive three full sets each, along with a pair of desert boots, a desert pattern cover for our kevlar helmets, two tee-shirts, two sweat cloths and some other knick-nacks that went with them. However, when the war finally started, it

117

was all over in one hundred hours. The day peace was declared, two forty-foot transit containers arrived in our location, full of our desert uniforms!

Once peace was finalised, instructions were issued for the return of personnel and equipment back to home bases in Europe. We asked our formation HQ about the hundreds of unused desert camouflage uniforms we now held and other such items as the fitness equipment, TVs and video machines, which were not in our unit's peacetime inventory.

Much to our horror we were instructed to dig a large pit and burn all these items. This sounded so ludicrous that we had the order verified twice. Ultimately the quartermaster was ordered to ensure that all the equipment that was not destroyed by fire was buried in a deep hole out in the desert and could never be used again.[77]

Not long after our return to the UK, a new conflict arose in the Middle East, which required the deployment of a peacekeeping force to protect a small ethnic minority from being slaughtered. I received a signal from our District Ordnance Branch instructing me to ensure that no desert pattern clothing was being held in the unit, as this was desperately needed for this new operational deployment. I was even ordered to search all barrack rooms, offices and stores to check that none had been brought back illegally.

From the time of our initial deployment we had battered the local HQ supply branch for a public address system that we could use around our vast sprawling unit. It eventually agreed to our request and a couple of weeks later we received a very high-tech American system. This was an immense computer-based, wire-free, radio system that allowed us to pre-record messages and alarms. We could position the speakers indoor or out and at any location we deemed suitable. We could also carry the smaller speakers with us if we so wished. It had been air-freighted from the USA especially for us. Total cost to the taxpayer-£125,000. The whole system was never unpacked, as again peace arrived too early.

This magnificent array of electronic wizardry joined the now unwanted desert clothing, the hundreds of unopened and undistributed parcels from the UK, and many many other pieces of equipment, in the burning pit.[78]

Gather Around, I Have Something to Say and it Won't Take Long

During another conflict our commanding officer deemed it necessary to impersonate Field Marshal Montgomery by addressing the whole unit each day to inform them what was going on. This is a task normally left to sub-unit commmanders, i.e. company commander down to section leader, after they have attended a formal unit 'O' group. To make things worse, this CO would stand outside his command post with everyone informally gathered around just feet away. Hence anyone more than two rows back could not hear a word he said and had to rely on their sub-unit commanders to glean what the hell was happening.

After experiencing a couple of these gatherings the RSM decided enough was enough and had a small wooden platform built for his leader to stand on during his performances in front of his troops. Nevertheless, as the colonel did not possess anything close to a drill sergeant's voice, he still could not be heard by those at the back. Perturbed by the whole display, the RSM scoured all the quartermaster's stores and found a hand-held megaphone that he hoped would aid the CO to project his voice. Before the next performance the RSM briefed his colonel on how to use this technicial instrument, i.e. by holding it in one hand just in front of his face and pressing a small switch when he wanted to talk.

The daily ritual began by the CO nearly injuring the people in the front row when he swung the megaphone around as he mounted the platform. He then commenced his customary and absurd daily briefing with such vastly important and ephemeral items as what time meals were and who was on guard duty that night. The only problem with this was that people at the back still could not hear what he was spouting on about, as he continually moved his head left and right while holding the megaphone stiffly in front of his chest.

After this attempt by the RSM to bolster the CO's image he was in utter despair but, using his vast knowledge of man-management, years of experience in dealing with the officer cadre and some direct speaking, he informed the CO, in such a way as to leave the officer to think that it was his idea, that forthwith there would be a daily Orders Group, held in the command post and attended by the sub-unit commanders only.

Soaps and War

While engaged in the art of fighting not everyone's waking moments are filled with the thought of killing, rape and pillage and one such person was a staff sergeant (SSgt) I knew. Back home in Blighty he was an avid watcher of TV soap operas, so much so that he had instructed his wife to videotape all episodes of his four favourite programmes while he was away.

When we returned from the conflict after many months, we were granted three weeks' leave and this staff sergeant went home to watch all the videos his wife had recorded so that he could catch up on the story lines. I have no idea how long it took him but he must have sat in front of his TV for hours on end each day.

To say that his peers classed him as a bit of a sad person would be putting it mildly. A year after his return from war he completed his twenty-two-year service and went out into Civvy Street. The last I heard about him was that he had failed to reach the minimum medical standards required to become a traffic warden.

The Biscuit Mutiny (Hearsay)

During an operational patrol in the Middle East a two-vehicle patrol stopped for the night out in the desert. The two pink-painted Land Rovers bristled with equipment, radios, machine guns, grenade launchers and personal equipment. As an informal Standing Operational Procedure all the food was carried in a metal box on the back of one of the vehicles (escape/emergency rations were carried by individuals).

The SNCO in charge of the patrol was called Geordie. He was a veteran of many campaigns but was now just going over the edge of operational viability.

Geordie took his map and compass and headed up the nearest sand dune to confirm their location.[79] On returning he saw that all the other lads were in a huddle around the food container.

'What's going on here then, lads?' says Geordie only to be met with mutters and whispers.

Going over to the second in charge he wanted to know what the problem was.

'Someone has been stealing rations', states the other SNCO.

'Right, let's get to the bottom of this straight away', and Geordie calls all the troops over. 'OK, lads what's wrong?'

'All the Garibaldi biscuits have gone', says one trooper near to tears.[80]

'Well, own up, who the hell has done this then?' demands Geordie, trying to sound authoritative.

In unison the troops reply, 'It's you Geordie.'

'I don't care who it is. It has to stop', screams Geordie as he strides away to the radio.

Bomb Run (Hearsay)

A few years ago the British Army assisted a Gulf state in its war against Communist insurgents who wanted to take over the southern end of the country. During this secretive, and even now not well-published, war, one of my comrades, Harry, was engaged in leading a company of local Firqas.[81]

Harry had been in the Army almost twenty-two years, most of this time spent in SF units of one kind or another. Not the most eloquent of soldiers, he was a hard taskmaster who always expected the best from those around him.

The Firqas, led by Harry, had chased a band of Adoo into a re-entry at the base of an escarpment but now found that they could not go in for the kill as the Adoo held the high ground and the Firqas were in relatively open ground. Harry decided to leave half his troops where they were and take the rest up onto the escarpment and attack from there.

While sitting on the cliff edge firing down into the Adoo position Harry made a tactical decision to call in an air-strike to bomb the enemy and finish off this action. The radio call went something like this:

'Red Leader this is Green Sixteen. Red Leader this is Green Sixteen. Mission for you. Over.'

'Green Sixteen this is Red Leader. Send details. Over.'

Harry then read off the details of the request as laid down in Standing Operating Procedures or SOPs.

'Green Sixteen this is Red Leader. Mission accepted and with you in fifteen minutes.'

Now Harry set about regrouping his Firqas so that they were not in direct danger of the intended air attack.

'Green Sixteen this is Red Leader. Five minutes out. Throw smoke.' Harry then ignited an orange smoke grenade to guide the plane in.

'Red Leader this is Green Sixteen. Orange smoke', called Harry into his radio and got the acknowledgement back form the pilot.

'Green Sixteen this is Red Leader. Two minutes out. Do you have me visual?' No reply.

'Green Sixteen. One minute out. Do you have me visual?' Again no reply.

'Green Sixteen. Thirty seconds out. Do you have me visual or I will abort?'

'Red Leader this is Green Sixteen. Don't know what you mean with all this visual crap but I can f*****g see you.'

The story goes that the poor old pilot had to call off this bombing run for laughter but once composed, he attempted it again but slightly changed the wording of his radio calls.

Morale-Boosting Visits

It has become the norm for political leaders, their wives and cohorts to visit war zones on morale-boosting visits. These can so easily backfire that they should be banned for all but the most senior and wise of the horde. I remember a very senior member of the British parliament visiting an Allied Forces camp and during a much published luncheon (shown live on American news channels) being asked if he liked the US Army MREs he had been served.[82]

'What do you think?' he answered, 'when MRE stands for Meals Refused by Ethiopians.'

During yet another high-powered visit we had to parade the unit so that a British political mandarin could drop in and justify his pre-Christmas duty-free jaunt around the world, all paid for with taxpayers' money of course. There we were, camping in a country that strictly controlled our dress code and social behaviour, banned us from drinking alcohol and would not allow us to openly celebrate Christmas. Yet this luminary arrived in a tatty, stained and rumpled cotton suit, only just able to stand, and with slurred speech tried to wish us all well in the forthcoming affray. As we had not been permitted to consume alcohol for some time, his whisky sodden breath was totally overpowering and his general demeanour, or lack of it, did nothing for our morale.

Don't Panic

We had been subjected to several air-raid warnings and a missile had missed our camp by only a half a mile on one occasion. The current threat appreciation indicated that the enemy had biological and chemical warheads and might use them, so we had to carry our NBC suits and respirators with us at all times.[83] The MoD had authorised the purchase civilian sports bags so that we could wander around the local towns, markets and bars and not draw too much attention to the fact that we had the equipment with us. The local government had refused to issue these items to the general public, either for monetary reasons or because they did not want any panic to set in.

No one had told us how we would be alerted to incoming nerve, blister or other chemical and biological agents when off duty. Nevertheless, should we be walking around the local market, or out sightseeing and noting people choking, twitching and dying all around us, we were to attempt to get our suits and respirators on as soon as possible. Little use really, as by the time you saw anyone fall convulsing to the floor it would be too late to act.

While on duty or in barracks, regular exercises were called and you just never knew if it was a test or the real thing. On one occasion I found myself in a bomb shelter trying to put my NBC kit on in total darkness. As the shelter was only thirty-six inches high and rather crowded, this usually slick routine was difficult at best and was not helped by the intense smothering heat from the midday sun. To make things worse, the person two down from me was whimpering and becoming more hysterical by the minute. In her panic to get to the air raid shelter she had forgotten to pick up her suit and respirator. As others around her settled down to check each other's equipment for mismatched seals and correct donning of suits, this woman was begging people to run out of the shelter to her office and return with her personal protection equipment. In a situation like this you find out who your friends are and who are the heroes. Needless to say, no one volunteered and she had to take her chances that this was in fact a drill and not the real thing.

When the all-clear was sounded and we slowly crawled out of our shelters, one very shamed faced and highly embarrassed QARANC captain wandered off to her office.[84]

Yet another incident happened during an air-raid practice and fortunately for the culprit it was only a practice. Our two senior officers had been given the use of two civilian cars for official purposes. What this meant to them was that they could use the staff cars for such journeys as to and from the beach club and sailing club, and to various barbeques and parties.

One day one of these lucky officers had parked his car outside the HQ complex and was sitting in his office when the air-raid warning sounded. At that same moment I was in the adjutant's office with the adjutant himself and two other people. Staying where we were, we started to put on our NBC suits and respirators and it was while carrying out this that we could hear someone running up and down the corridor and getting more frantic with each turn. Soon that person was screaming and shouting, and it was then that we recognised the owner of the voice. Much to our embarrassment (and pleasure) it became obvious that the person was acting in a manner much unbecoming an officer and gentleman and every second word was a harsh expletive.

We continued with our own personal drills and prepared to carry out Standing Operational Procedures (SOPs) as laid down for such situations, i.e. emergency actions on the unit being hit by a missile-possibly contaminated with biological or chemical agents. As we did so, the door to the adjutant's office was flung open and a red-faced, sweaty, and highly animated major charged in. The poor thing had heard the siren go off and instantly looked around for his NBC equipment. Not immediately locating it as he should have been able to do, he had suddenly realised that he had left it in the boot of his civilian staff car and, to make things worse, he could find neither the driver nor car keys.

To compound the whole thing, a few days later a private soldier was spotted without his NBC kit and was marched in front of the said major who awarded the poor individual a £200 stoppage of pay.[85]

Don't Take it Too Seriously

Prior to deploying to one conflict we paraded outside Regimental HQ so that the RSM could inspect his troops, brief us on last-minute changes and ensure that all were present. As the RSM marched through the ranks checking for correct dress and equipment, the parade was joined by some of the officers who were to travel with us. The RSM's usual immaculate parade-ground manners were abruptly curtailed when he noticed that some of the officers carried non-regulation items with them.

Two captains had fishing rods and other angling equipment, while one other and two lieutenants had plastic buckets and spades attached to their webbing. As the RSM marched over to speak to these officers, he was overheard asking what the hell they thought they were doing. One captain replied that as they were going off to a desert scenario they thought that they would lighten up the seriousness of the deployment by carrying their little toys. Just a good wheeze and all very good for the enlisted ranks' morale ,etc., etc.

After as short sharp address by the RSM and a few well-chosen words from the second-in-command, the officers concerned removed the offending items and were rather subdued and crestfallen as they climbed aboard the transport.

Hard Night, Ma'am?

During the early part of the build-up to a recent war we were fortunate enough to be billeted in five-star hotels on an island in the

Persian Gulf. As the concentration of troops increased we were allocated different hotels based upon gender, rank and the perceived prestige of the hotel concerned. Senior male officers were generally accommodated in the Sheraton, female officers in the Hilton, while junior male officers and warrant officers were in the Inter-continental. Senior NCOs and other ranks were billeted in local hotels. Incidentally, RAF aircrews, pilots and navigators, were with the female officers in the Hilton and of course there was no comment made about that.

As we were not allowed to move around independently in uniform, we were picked up from outside our hotels and conveyed to and from the unit's location by contracted local buses. One morning our bus had to call at the Hilton to pick up the female officers. One or two of these had obviously had a hard night in the bar or disco the night before and were given a good ribbing about this when they boarded the bus.

A staff sergeant noted something wrong with one of the female officers as she sat down and in a loud voice asked, 'Ma'am, did you get up late or out of the wrong side of the bed today?'

'No,' she replied, 'why do you ask?'

'Nothing really. But I couldn't help noticing that you're wearing RAF pilot's boots this morning.'

What an Embarrassment

As we prepared to move towards the battlefront we had to hand over our present location to an allied army unit. After much paperwork and endless checking and re-checking of the equipment to be left behind, we finally got to the very last briefing during which we would officially relinquish the location and a sort of ceremony of the keys would take place.

Our commanding officer chaired the briefing and the allied unit's senior personnel sat in. All was going well until the CO suddenly began crying and collapsed out of his chair, beating his head and fists on the floor. Most of us, including the foreigners, sat mortified-in-our seats wondering what the hell was going on, while our second in command and adjutant helped the CO out of the room.

After a very embarrassing fifteen or twenty minutes, the adjutant rejoined us and explained that the CO had been taken back to his billets as he was unwell. The brief, which was now chaired by the 2i/c, was cut short but the handover completed. Later that day, as we boarded the transport to our new location, I spoke to the adjutant about the CO's indisposition and he enlightened me as to what had caused the emotional outburst.

Evidently the CO liked to speak to his wife, who was back in the UK, every evening and this had become a sort of ritual that he went out of his way to maintain at the same time each day. Unfortunately he had been unable to get through to her the previous evening and it had weighed heavily on his mind this morning.

My God! This man had missed one phone call home and practically had a nervous breakdown because of it. What the hell would it be like when the going got tough and he was leading us into battle?

Let's Get Moving

Not really a story about war or conflict, this anecdote refers to disaster relief.

One Saturday afternoon I had retired to a local pub and was enjoying a beer when in rushed the CO's driver. He informed me that I had to return to the unit, as soon as possible, as we had been detailed to mobilise personnel for emergency deployment to the Indian subcontinent after an earthquake there.

Fifteen minutes later I was back at the unit lines and briefed-up on the current state of affairs. I was then given the task of recalling personnel known to be away on courses, leave and other absences. Someone else had the task of rounding up personnel that were supposed to be in the local area.[86]

Many of the contacts were easy to trace and I soon had personnel en route back to the unit; however, some were totally out of reach and did not ring back for hours and even days. Others just could not grasp the urgency of the situation, and as sure as eggs are eggs, it was the officers who proved the hardest to get motivated.

One junior officer was traced to his family's home and within minutes I had him on the phone and briefed that he had to be back in the unit by first thing the next morning. This gave him fourteen hours to travel overnight, from the other end of the country, pack his kit and be at the CO's briefing by 0830 hours, and ready to deploy straight after that.

Despite that, he plagued me with questions about what money he needed to bring, what major banks were in the country and would there be facilities available to exchange travellers' cheques, etc. Anyway, I must admit to telling him the odd fib in an attempt to get him off the telephone and moving back to his unit.

Another officer was not so easy to deal with. He wanted to know whether he should bring a lounge suit and his Mess dress uniform. Asked why he would possibly think that he would need such clothing when he was being deployed on an emergency humanitarian support mission, he spent several minutes explaining that he did not want to arrive there and find that he had not packed the correct dress for any formal Officers' Mess functions that might take place.

My answer went something like this: 'Excuse me, sir, but I really don't think that any Mess functions are planned, nor do I expect that any Officers' Messes out there, if there are any, will be bothered with such silly things, considering what has just happened to their country.'

'Sergeant Major, I'm not sure that I like your tone and will be speaking to the colonel when I see him tomorrow', was his reply.

'See you at 0830 hours tomorrow, sir', I concluded, and put the phone down.

When the said officer arrived, he did go and complain to the commanding officer about my alleged insubordination. But when the CO heard the story, he ripped several layers off the officer and promptly told him to apologise to me personally for his stupidity and ineptitude. This he did, rather shamefaced but politely.

Time For a Smoke

A very good friend of mine, who had served many tours in Northern Ireland at the height of the Troubles, would only ever smoke cigarettes that he had hand-rolled himself. I was thus duty bound to ask him why.

He told me that on one particular night-time foot patrol through a very rough and unfriendly district of Belfast in the early 1970s, the junior NCO in charge of the patrol passed a message along the line of men to take a five-minute break in the doorways of the houses on either side of the terraced street. One of the less experienced soldiers, and a very good mate of my friend's, decided that five minutes was just long enough for a quick crafty smoke.[87] Having pulled out a cigarette he was just about to light it with his lighter, when a single shot rang out and he dropped dead on the spot, having been hit in the head by a sniper's round.

It was therefore my comrade's thinking that if his friend had only smoked hand-rolled cigarettes he would not have had time to smoke one during that fatal patrol and would subsequently have lived to see the day out.

The Territorial Army

If you were lucky enough to be one of the chosen few you got posted to the Territorial Army, or TAVR, to give it its full title.[88] You would more than likely have been sent there as a Permanent Staff Instructor (PSI) and usually on a three-year tour, either training the TA personnel or working in such appointments as the RSM or RQMS.

Many people will tell you that these are plum jobs, much sought after by people keen to further their career. The truth is that most PSIs hate the job and cannot wait to get back to the real Army. Very few actually manage to make great leaps up the promotion ladder; some do but the majority just get one rank further, if they keep that. And there are numerous accounts of PSIs returning to the regular Army reduced in rank after a run in with a TA officer; personality and not performance is the usual byword in these circumstances.

The most common complement of PSIs in a unit would be a senior officer as CO and perhaps another officer as adjutant or training officer, the RSM or RQMS, maybe a PSI, or perhaps both. You may get SNCOs as detachment sergeants or running the MT pool. This varies greatly but you will certainly be in the minority and, in some cases, disliked for just being a PSI.

Most TA units are very sharp and professional, but when you find a bad one they are very bad. Some are no more than glorified drinking clubs. The one I was sent to was definitely the worst unit I worked with in all my twenty-four years.

In this unit the CO was TA, as was his brother who was also the second-in-command, his sister was married to the TA quartermaster, whose nephew was a TA company sergeant major and so it went on.

We had a PSI captain as training officer/adjutant, a PSI as RSM, me as the PSI RQMS, a staff sergeant as PSI 2i/c of the transport section, a PSI staff sergeant as unit chief clerk and two lance corporals as PSI drivers.

As a PSI you were expected to attend every day, Monday to Friday (0830-1630 hours), plus every Drill Night (1930-2200 hours) and all training weekends.[89]

Generally when a TA unit does well all the praise goes to the TA personnel; when things go wrong its the PSI's fault.

Absent Friends

One of the first things I noticed was that the quartermaster (QM) never appeared during the Drill Nights.[90] When I went around the unit I also noted that the 2i/c was absent every Drill Night as well. As the RSM was away almost permanently on resettlement courses, I went to the PSI adjutant/training officer and asked him about this. He had been with the unit only a few months but informed me that the two officers did actually attend but on a different evening to the Drill Nights. They also attended some weekends but only if we were going to stay in camp. He further informed me that if I wanted to leave any paperwork or messages for the QM, I should either put them on his desk or in his mailbox.

It transpired that the two officers, who would be classed as key figures in the running of any regular unit, would come into the TA centre, book themselves in for an evening and then spend most of the time drinking cheap booze in the Officers' Mess.

After a few months I started marking files and letters in the QM's in-tray to see if he actually came into the office at all. Much to my surprise very little was moved around between the in-and out-trays on an evening. In my first three months I saw the QM only twice and one of those was when I worked late one evening.

Senior NCOs on Parade

The 2i/c and QM were not the only two who turned up and did nothing. We had a problem with the SNCOs, as they would attend muster parade with the unit at the beginning of the Drill Night and then drift off to the Sergeants' Mess without attending any of the training or administration periods.

In an attempt to stop this, we (the hated PSIs) instituted a system of signing-in, whereby all personnel attending a training period, lecture, admin duty, etc., had to sign an attendance sheet. These would be checked at the end of the Drill Night and we also carried out spot checks on who was attending what training during the Drill Night.

We also insisted that all SNCOs and warrant officers attended a dismissal parade at the end of the evening. This ensured that all the personnel that started the Drill Night were still there at the end. In the absence of an RSM, I as the senior warrant officer in the unit closed the Mess bar until after the dismissal parade.

That Puts a New Light On It

As I lacked an effective departmental boss, i.e. the quartermaster, I had to fumble through on my own. The Army in its wisdom had plucked me from a regular Army unit in Central America to become the RQMS of a TA unit in Scotland. I had no formal training as an RQMS, had never worked in supply and logistics before and therefore had to sit and read all the numerous manuals on how to do the job. The DOWO[91] at District HQ was very helpful; initially sympathetic to my plight, he would, quite naturally get slightly exasperated with my thrice-daily telephone calls for advice, assistance and divine guidance.

I had to quickly learn the ropes. One thing that became plainly obvious was that as the PSI RQMS, all the unit equipment was effectively in my charge. I therefore set about a hundred per cent audit of the inventories. This included vehicles, weapons, tentage, clothing, office furniture, radios and the hundreds of nuts and bolts that allow a military unit to function. All adding up to several hundreds of thousands of pounds, if not millions.

During this check I was unable to locate a field generator and its associated lighting equipment. Try as I did, I could not find them anywhere in the unit nor could I find any paperwork to say that they had been moved elsewhere. I broached the subject with the PSI adjutant hoping that he might know something about it. He gave me

133

a rather knowing nod and closed the office door so that we could speak in private. He told me that the CO lived outside the city in a secluded house miles from the main road. Rather than pay the electricity board a small fortune to wire the house to the national grid, he used the generator and lighting equipment to power the house.

Your Wheels-My Work

Not long after arriving I had to go to District HQ for an interview with my respective District Commander.[92] Off I went to speak to the PSI staff sergeant in charge of transport. I wanted to use the unit car for this journey and, as there was no training going on, it should have been available. Confronting the staff sergeant in his office with this request I received a sad nodding of his head and a 'tut tut' in reply.

'What's wrong?' I said. 'Don't tell me you have it in for servicing or something else.'

'Sir. You'll learn that it is never available unless the colonel requests it', explained the staff sergeant. 'Perhaps you have never noticed but it is very rarely here, as is one of my PSI lance corporals.'

Asking him to explain further I learnt that, with the CO's permission, one of the PSI lance corporals was tasked everyday to be on call in case the 2i/c wanted to use the staff car for personal or business matters. This had been going on for some years and must have used many gallons of MoD fuel as well.

There was no way I could ignore this gross abuse of power, nor did I want to directly upset my new commanding officer (or his brother, the second-in-command). So after several lengthy conversations with other RQMSs and many hours poring over Material Regulations for the Army, I contacted my friendly DOWO at HQ. Informally, I hinted at the possible abuse but also directed him to the regulations for the allocation of staff cars to TA units. It became clear that we were not entitled to a staff car and in no time at all, the 2i/c had lost his personal taxi and the unit gained a much valued minibus.

Free Uniforms for All

Each Drill Night our unit recruiting team was available to interview any new recruits and to get them to take the Queen's shilling by signing on for TA service. The only problem here is that one vast difference between the Regular Army and the TA is that with the TA you can just stop playing any time. You are supposed to return any equipment you were issued and the unit will send you a short letter about the Official Secrets Act-end of story.

I did notice that we always seemed to have plenty of potential recruits around and occasionally we ran formal recruit training weekends. Nevertheless, the number of recruits never seemed to match up to the vast number of potential new boys and I wondered why. Another thing that I noted was the large amount of clothing that was being written off each month.[93]

It came to my attention that a reason for the large number of potential recruits each week was that they were being issued a full scale of clothing and equipment on their first night. Having signed for all this, they departed into the darkness and were never seen again.

How many young people in our catchment area had army boots for work? How many had a full set of combat clothing for gardening or fishing? How much could you get for a set of webbing down at the local car boot sale?

After a protracted and meaningful argument with the unit's recruiting officer it was decided that we would only issue recruits with a set of coveralls, a cap and a pair of boots until they proved that they were serious about joining the TA.

Guns at Twenty Paces

One of the most unfortunate things about the TA is that you can have some of the older generation of officers still on board. For the most part many have never come to grips with the fact that Kitchener has already left for India or that Queen Victoria has died.

This fact was rammed home to me on one my first training weekends when I had to go to the firing ranges with this TA unit. We had deployed so those members of the unit who had not carried out their annual range classification could do so. Soldiers had to qualify with their personal weapons which were either the 7.62mm Self-Loading Rifle (SLR) or 9mm Sub-Machine Gun (SMG), while the officers used the 9mm Browning pistol.

I had the task of running the 9mm pistol range and was generally horrified at the appalling standard of the range safety, weapon handling and basic shooting skills of the officers. Many could not strip down and assemble the weapon, some did not know how to load a magazine and with others the safest place on the range when they were firing was directly in front of the target.

Late in the morning the 2i/c condescended to show up and wanted to carry out his range classification. Regrettably this led to a face to face stand off between us, as I would not let him shoot on the range dressed as he was. With no combat jacket or trousers on, he had turned up in barrack dress and leather-soled parade shoes. With a chance that he might slip over on the grass range and possibly shoot someone, I refused to allow him onto the firing point. My decision was backed up by our PSI adjutant who, with all due respect for rank, told the Major that if he wished to qualify he should go home and change his dress to something more suitable for range work. Muttering things about 'Bloody PSIs' and 'Why do we need them' he stormed off, and returned two or three hours later demanding to shoot.

Having spent time showing him how to load, unload, make ready and make safe the weapon, I instructed the 2i/c to come onto the firing point and shoot off six rounds just to get used to firing the weapon. However, this did not quite go according to plan. As I told the officer to adopt a firing position and he did so, I fell about the range laughing.

With left leg straight, right knee bent to ninety degrees and facing side on to the target, he had placed his left hand on his hip and with the pistol in his right hand, had taken a stance more in keeping with someone attempting a thrust or lunge in fencing.

Danger, Man at Work

Having finished my range work for the day, I went over to watch the soldiers on the SLR range only to find that the Skill at Arms instructor running this classification was having major problems with one particular soldier. The young lad had the terrifying habit of turning round on the firing point and had more than once ended up facing completely the wrong way with a loaded weapon in his hand.

As all the others had qualified with this weapon, the instructor decided to give the young soldier some personal coaching. But even with the instructor standing just behind him he still swung the rifle around as if at a wild turkey shoot. Despairing, the instructor pulled the soldier off the firing point and unloaded the weapon. He then disappeared into the range hut and was heard cutting timber and knocking nails into wood.

When he reappeared he carried a wooden rectangular frame, akin to a picture frame with two long handles on one side. Taking the soldier back onto the firing point, he positioned the frame over the man's head onto his chest. Now, standing behind him and holding the handles, the instructor could maintain him in a safe position.

Recruiting Display in Town

It was decided by the commanding officer that the unit recruiting team would mount a display in the town market place one Saturday to create a higher unit profile. So off went the team and came back three weeks later with their plans for this event. Leaflets and posters would be displayed in all prominent places in the town and articles printed in the local newspapers informing the populace.

We were to have static displays of vehicles and equipment, a mobile small-bore range was to be built on the back of a four-tonne lorry and a selection of weapons displayed in a tent. The usual posters, pamphlets and videos would be available to show what the TA got up to and the recruiting team would be there to sign up any potential new members.

Of course all the PSIs would be involved and one of the only things we were worried about was security for the event. Not only for the participants but also for the equipment, especially the weapons they wanted to display. We insisted that the local constabulary be kept well informed of this event and that they ensure an overt presence around the area throughout the day. Unfortunately, organisations like the IRA would love to have easy access to this sort of thing, not to mention such groups as CND or the Welsh Free Army (Viet Taff as we knew them).

Once the CO grasped the dire consequences of any security lapse, he placed the quartermaster in charge of security, not that there was the slightest chance that the QM would even appear at the display. The QM overreacted in his usual non-military way and insisted that all the PSIs be armed with pistols and live ammunition in case we were attacked, bombed or caught someone stealing equipment.[94] Of course when the police heard about this they were not too amused and insisted that the display be held in the TA Centre instead, with all visitors searched as they entered.

Dedication to Duty

Our annual summer camp was divided into two parts. The first week was dedicated to military training and the second week was for such adventurous pursuits as rock climbing, abseiling, canoeing, mountain bike rides, and sailing. I was more concerned with the first week as we had a three-day exercise planned. This started with a long night-time drive from one side of the country to the other, with all the unit vehicles in convoy. Once there we set up a tactical location and mounted perimeter guards and set out nuclear, biological and chemical warfare detection equipment. Next day we practised mock air-raids and infantry attacks on our position. Recce parties were sent out and the camouflage of vehicles and tentage constantly checked and improved.

As night fell all section commanders and their second-in-commands were given a briefing for a tactical night move to another location. This would include an eight-hour drive on motorways, country roads and across country. At the appointed hour all the camouflage was taken down, equipment stored away and vehicles lined up for the move. As per Unit Standing Operating Procedures, all personnel and weapons were checked before we departed.

The night move went without too many hitches and we moved into the new location just as dawn was breaking. The senior TA warrant officer was acting RSM for this exercise and he was responsible for perimeter security, for ensuring that guards were set out and given its arcs of fire and areas of responsibility. It was my responsibility to check that he was doing this correctly, so we walked around the perimeter to check each slip trench together.

Alas, one of the positions was not manned so we went in search of the section commander responsible. He informed us that he was still trying to locate the personnel who had manned the guard trenches prior to our move. Hunting around the whole location we were unable to find them and could only come to the conclusion that they had been left at the last location. Having explained this to our headquarters, I was given permission to take a Land Rover and one of the PSI drivers to return to the old location. Cutting off the corners and heading straight there, we arrived around midday. As we drove into the location we spotted two armed and camouflaged figures peering out from a trench. When we approached one cocked his rifle, shouted for us to halt and challenged us for the password.

'Don't be bloody stupid', I shouted. 'Where the hell do you think the rest of the unit has gone.'

Still challenging us (surprisingly using the correct procedure), I gave in and replied with yesterday's password. This brought the two men out of their trench and I told them to sit down and relax.

'Did you not notice the whole unit driving out of here last night?' I questioned.

'Yes, but no one told us to stand down or to abandon our post. So we thought that you would be coming back', said one.

'The RSM told us not to leave the trench for any reason whatsoever and that he would ensure that we were relieved for meals and at the end of our guard duty', said the other.

While these two had a brew of tea, my driver radioed back to HQ that we had found the missing men and I took the opportunity to walk around the now deserted location. I found one gas stove, a sleeping bag, two camouflage nets still hanging from trees, a pair of binoculars and the working parts from inside a 9mm pistol.

Returning to the new location I reported into the headquarters with my two wayward strays. The CO went ballistic with them until I interjected. At least these two soldiers had performed all the duties asked of them, even if they were a bit stupid, but I wanted to get hold of the their section commander who had told me that he had accounted for all his personnel before we left the last location. I also wanted to find the officer carrying a 9mm pistol without any working parts inside it.

A Dry Weekend

Later on during my time with this TA unit, I was tasked with arranging a weekend camp at a training area some hundreds of miles from our base. The objectives to be achieved were convoy-driving discipline, radio-operator training, cross-country driver training and, as a treat for all, section attacks using live ammunition and live hand grenade throwing. To achieve the last tasks I had used my contacts in the Paras to get a couple of instructors to assist our Skill at Arms men.

This is not the sort of thing that you can organise on the back of a cigarette pack. Ammunition has to be ordered and collected. Rations demanded, fuel allocated and detailed orders issued. On the Drill Night prior to this specific weekend I held a full briefing for all those officers, SNCOs and departmental heads involved. Everything seemed to be falling into place, we were scheduled to depart Friday evening at 2000 hours and return to barracks by 1800 hours Sunday. We hoped that the weather would be kind to us and everyone would have an enjoyable training weekend.

Returning to my office after the briefing I settled down to complete my personal preparations and to sort out any other business that had occurred in my short absence. Just before the Drill Night finished the HQ company sergeant major (CSM) knocked on my door. He stated that all the equipment and stores were loaded and all except the last vehicle were back in the garages.

'Shall I send the last four-tonne around to the back of the Sergeants' Mess and load up from there?' he asked.

'Load what?' I inquired, knowing that I had not asked for any stores from the Mess.

'The bar stocks', he intoned. 'Beer, spirits, soft drinks, etc.'

'Do you really think that I'm going to allow you lot to drink yourselves silly then go out and drive cross country at night or even worse, to shoot and throw live grenades while still under the influence of alcohol? No way. No bar, no beer, no alcohol, full stop. This is a military training weekend not a beach party. If it wasn't in my deployment instructions it's not going. Understood?'

'But we always take a bar with us on this sort of training', he implored.

'Not when I have been with you and certainly not when my signature is on all the safety instructions', I commanded. 'Now get that vehicle in the garages and the dismissal parade formed up for the adjutant.'

That evening in the Sergeants' Mess, where we would meet up for a few drinks after a Drill Night, I detected a very frosty atmosphere when I walked in.

Friday evening I was in early and all ready for the move off to the training weekend. As 2000 hours approached I went out to the form-up area. As always, all the other PSIs were there, but only six TA members.

'Where the hell are the rest of them?' the adjutant asked.

'Don't know, sir', said the MT staff sergeant. 'They all knew they were supposed to be here for a 2000 hours move.'

'Ohh, sir,' interrupted one of the TA chaps, a corporal who had been with the unit for twenty-six years, 'I don't think many will turn up this weekend.'

'Why's that then?' I asked.

''Cause there's no bar', he explained.

True to his word, only the six TA soldiers attended that evening and we, the PSIs, had the embarrassing task of calling around all the other agencies concerned to cancel the training, return the ammo and food, and apologise for any inconvenience caused.

Crooks or What?

For a TA soldier to quit his unit and terminate his commitment with the TA, the only thing he has to do is to hand in his uniform and personal equipment, and he can then disappear into the night. The unit will eventually send him some paperwork about the Official Secrets Act but he is a free man otherwise.

One day I was sitting at my desk trying to work out what to do with some complicated piece of paperwork, when an elderly gentleman appeared at the office door asking if he could drop off the kitbag he held. Before I could ask him who he was, he had gone. Searching through the kitbag, which contained various pieces of uniforms and webbing, I found a name and realised that the kit belonged to one of our long-serving TA staff sergeants who had suddenly decided to finish with the TA. After discussing this with the RSM (on one of the very few days that he was in the unit lines), we came to the conclusion that there must be a very good reason for this sudden loss of heart and for the staff sergeant to quit. We therefore carried out an immediate one hundred per cent check of all the equipment and stores that this man had held just before his departure. Lo and behold, we found that several expensive items were missing.

We made several telephone calls to his home and workplace, but none were returned. Finally, we called in our friendly local policeman, who along with our PSI staff sergeant, went around to the man's home. When they arrived he was not there but his wife opened the door. She very kindly, or naively, allowed our men to look through the garage and cellar, where her husband had kept his military kit. Here they found most of the missing items and a few that we did not know were missing, including a complete tent and a range of cooking equipment. All this information was passed up the chain of command within the unit but I never heard anything official about the outcome.

On another occasion I was standing in the command post during a winter exercise and made a comment that we could actually do with some kind of heating, perhaps something like the bottled gas heater that doubles up as a light. The next thing I know is that a TA sergeant walks into my office and tells me that he has left some equipment with the storeman downstairs. He said that he couldn't stay as he was actually still at work for a national utility company and his bosses would miss him if he was away too long. My curiosity eventually got the better of me and I went to see what he had left. To my surprise I found a large Calor gas heater/light.

A week or so later I had a phone call from someone at the utility company asking if they could drop round and see me on a personal matter. The chap was accompanied by a detective sergeant and they asked about items that had gone missing from their company's stores; they thought I might be able to help recover some of these. One of the items was a Calor gas heater/light.

When the police raided the TA sergeant's house they found a large stockpile of spades, pickaxes and other implements used by the utility company plus as much, if not more, Army clothing and equipment as I held in my stores.

Chicken Legs

It is a long-established tradition within the British Army units for the officers, warrant officers and SNCOs to wait at table during the Junior Ranks Christmas Dinner and in this the TA is no different from Regular Army units.

As I went round serving food and drink to the hordes of soldiers, many of whom were never seen from one Christmas dinner to the next, one observation was continually made and that was that as usual no one had been served a chicken leg. This started me thinking and I consciously noted all the meals on the tables and it was true. There was plenty of white breast meat but not one leg or wing to be seen. During a short respite in the activities I broached the subject with one of the TA SNCOs. He had served for over twenty years in the TA and was one of the few that you could rely upon. He told me that at all the dinners he had attended he had never seen a chicken leg. He also enlightened me with the fact that the chefs (who came under the direct command and control of the quartermaster) always purchased all the unit's food supplies from the same retailer and had done so for as long as he could remember. In fact, he informed me that the QM and master chef received substantial hampers from the retailer every Christmas.

Not overly impressed with this, I went and tackled the master chef. He was a TA staff sergeant who had served with the unit for nearly as long as his very good drinking buddy, the QM. He reinforced the information I had received from the sergeant, 'That is the way it is and that was the way it had always been.'

Still not totally won over, I hung around the unit lines until later that night. As the diners finished their meals, they retired to the unit bar, while the chefs cleared everything away and finally departed. As the master chef and one of his minions headed to his car I noted that they carried two large black plastic bags. I was more than a little intrigued as to what was in them, so I shouted the staff sergeant's name and headed across the now dark car park towards them. They immediately dropped the bags, jumped in the car and sped out of the barracks.

True to my gut feelings, the bags contained a veritable hoard of pillaged food, which was held as evidence when the two men appeared before the commanding officer on formal disciplinary procedures (much against the protestations of the QM I must add).

I never did find out what the real reason was for the absence of all those chicken legs.

What a Cracking Party

Our PSI captain (adjutant/training officer) was due to move on to better and greater things, so a relief was posted in. The new chap was a transfer in from a cavalry regiment and this was to be his first appointment within this Cap Badge.[95]

As is usual in such situations a small party was organised by the TA personnel to bid farewell to the old hand and to welcome the new appointment holder. Unfortunately, after the two guests of honour left, this small gathering became a large and unruly mob. Lamp fittings and curtains were pulled down, carpets soaked in spilt drinks and vomit, furniture was broken and some rather saucy antics were caught on camera.

Next morning was the new adjutant/training officer's first day in post and he was not too impressed with the fallout from the night before. Fortunately none of the other PSIs was involved in the previous evening's shindig and the commanding officer directed that the new incumbent be left to carry out a full investigation, apportion blame and mete out disciplinary action as necessary.

Having never worked in a TAVR environment before the poor chap became totally exasperated with the whole thing. No one would own up to anything or put the finger on anyone else. Witnesses dried up, some claiming to have been blind drunk or in the toilets when things had happened.

By the end of his first week in office this PSI officer was totally distraught by the whole affair. He got little backing from his (supposed) fellow officers; the TA Sergeants' Mess members were against any form of action; and the junior ranks didn't care much either way, as they would just simply go home and resign from the TAVR if they were implicated in any way.

By the end of the second week the officer concerned had reported sick to the local hospital and was last seen being escorted onto a shuttle flight south, so that he could be admitted to a military hospital for psychiatric evaluation and therapy. The previous holder of this office was called back from leave and his posting delayed until a 'suitable' replacement could be found.

Weapon Cleaning

We received instructions from District Headquarters that our annual Ordnance Inspection would take place in a few weeks' time. This was to concentrate on our holding of personal weapons and their ancillary items such as bayonets, slings, cleaning kits, etc. Having carried out monthly checks on these I had no hestation that I, as the RQMS, could account for everything we should have. The only aspect that worried me was the actual cleanliness of the weapons themselves.

I asked our PSI adjutant if, during the Drill Night immediately prior to the inspection, we could get all the weapons out of the armoury and have the unit personnel thoroughly clean them. He agreed wholeheartedly but said that he would have to inform the CO. No problems, I thought, but how wrong I was again. The CO insisted that Drill Nights were for his unit members to carry out personal administration, clothing and equipment exchanges, and for briefings on the forthcoming training weekends. Not for wholesale weapons cleaning.

So I personally approached the CO about this and asked if we could use time during a training weekend between then and the inspection to clean the weapons. It would take only an hour out of the programme at the most, I pleaded. No, came the answer, the only weekends available were planned for radio training and voice procedures, map reading and an orienteering competition, not to mention an Officers' Mess curry afternoon, and he wasn't going to mess up the programme. Just need one hour I beseeched him-to no avail

The PSIs, he claimed, were in the unit each day and in his opinion we didn't seem to have much to do most of the time. So he ordered me to get them to do the weapon cleaning, which we did. We spent days stripping apart, cleaning and oiling, then reassembling rifles, sub-machine guns and pistols, plus all their magazines and bayonets.

Some weeks later the CO read out, to the whole unit on parade, a letter, from District HQ, which went to great lengths to commend the commanding officer and his TA unit for the extremely high standard of all the weapons presented at the recent Ordnance Inspection.

Another glowing report and gold star for the TA-Sod the poor PSI.

Get Me Out of Here

After the fiasco of the training weekends, added to the general unpro-fessionalism, incompetence, and total mismanagement of the unit, compounded by the event described above, I had to get out of this unit for my own sanity and military career.

Trying to talk the situation over with the senior PSI in the unit, the captain who held the dual appointments of adjutant and training officer, was more than a little difficult, as he was totally preoccupied with how he could keep his wife from finding out about his girlfriend. She (the girlfriend) just happened to be one of the full-time civilian clerks in the unit orderly room. So I decided to use my prerogative as a warrant officer and ask for a personal interview with my respective commander at District HQ. As I had already met him on several occasions, including during my arrivals interview, and having supplied him, over the telephone, with a very basic outline of the problem, he granted my request for a personal interview the very next day. He also insisted that due to the sensitive nature of the matter in hand neither my CO nor any other unit officer would be informed of this appointment. If anyone asked I was just going for a routine visit to HQ.

When I arrived for the interview the commander seemed to be well versed and totally up to date with the appalling state of the unit. None the less, after listening to me for over an hour he asked me what I, personally, wanted to do about the situation. I immediately asked him for a posting to another unit, as I feared that I might ruin my career if I stayed where I was (this included my concern that I might end up punching the CO, etc.). The commander was extremely sympathetic, and as I sat in his office he telephoned my manning and records office requesting an immediate non-disciplinary posting. Regardless of the reason for the request, the only posting available meant me losing my acting rank of Warrant Officer Class Two. Two weeks later I arrived at my new unit as a staff sergeant and, as they say, the rest is history.

The district commander ordered a full and urgent investigation into the unit. This investigation resulted, fourteen months later, with the unit being disbanded and any TA soldier wishing to stay on was absorbed into other local TAVR units. The remaining PSIs were only too pleased to be released of the TA burden and returned to the Regular Army. The commanding officer, second-in-command and quartermaster were asked to resign their TA commissions.

Conclusion

Reorganise to Reorganise

One of the great mysteries of service life has to be the constant reorganisation that goes on. During my time we went from Districts to Divisions to Commands to Field Forces and back again. Each successive government seems to think it knows best and the mandarins in Whitehall spend millions of pounds and years of so-called research devising ways to save money and manpower, while wasting valuable resources reorganising the whole shooting match.

A classic example has to be the airborne unit I served in for a while. In April 1977 the unit was disbanded as it was deemed superfluous to the modern Army concept as laid down in the 1975 Defence Review. The unit had had a short but glorious history dating back to its conception in July 1942. It saw action in France, Italy, Greece and Palestine. It was twice deployed to Cyprus and twice to Egypt. Borneo was a long-term posting for the unit as well.

However, following Operation Corporate (the retaking of the Falkland Islands in 1982), it was decided that the Airborne Brigade needed such a unit again, so on 1 April 1985 the unit was re-formed. Yet in 1999 the unit was again disbanded as the new Air Assault Brigade was formed and the unit was again no longer needed.

Another fine example must have been the phased redundancy programme started in the early 1990s. Introduced because someone at the MoD, possibly chivvied along by well-meaning civil servants at the Treasury, considered that the perceived threat from the former Soviet Union had diminished sufficiently so that we did not need an army of its current size. So personnel, of all ranks and from nearly all regiments, corps, cap badges and trades, were invited to apply for early retirement (if you were commissioned officer) or redundancy (if you were an enlisted soldier). When this did not draw the required numbers, compulsory retirement or redundancy was forced on many. The older, longer serving, or those considered to have reached their ceiling were thrown out under this scheme. Experience counted for nothing.

The people who authorised this dreadful idea must have been so ill-informed that it was lamentable, or had they just failed to understand that units going on operational tours to such places as Northern Ireland, Belize, Hong Kong and Cyprus were already so under-manned that commanding officers were forced to beg, steal and borrow individuals, platoons, companies and squadrons from other units to bring the units up to the minimum operational deployment manning levels?

Yet a few short years later I read that the Army is suffering from major overstretch and under-manning and that compulsory call-up for the TA may have to be introduced to cover the shortfall.

Resettlement

After 24 years and 97 days my time in the Regular Army came to its end. What a great time I had had. I'd seen most of the world, worked with some fantastic organisations and individuals. I had learnt so much, while being privileged to have seen and done things that most people can only imagine.

Like all regular military personnel I had to undergo Resettlement Training for my move into civilian life. I will not say 'back into civilian life' as I do not consider that I had ever been there before. I joined as a spotty fifteen-year-old just out of school. I had never really worked in civilian employment, so I did not know what it was all about.

The Services tries hard to retrain, reprogramme and reorientate its workforce. You will find generals doing building and plastering courses prior to leaving so that they can work on their plush new civilian houses. You will find people like me attempting to learn all about computers, a beast that I kept well away from in the Army. You can go on courses and seminars to learn how to manage people the civilian way, without shouting and screaming at them or being able to put them in jail for a few days.

What the vast majority of ex-servicemen have to offer any employer is loyalty, dedication to a task and its correct completion, honesty and integrity, plus the ability to think through a problem, come to a successful conclusion and be able to organise how it is best attained.

Even so, some servicemen and women do not adjust to civilian life too well. They lose contact with the mates they have had for many years. They miss the companionship and unfailing trust that builds up over time. Many a story exists about people leaving the forces after years of faithful service, who find that they are now considered too old, at forty, to start a second career. So they turn to drink or become clinically depressed. A number have been known to commit suicide or just simply to have curled up and died.

This wasn't going to happen to me, so I spent the last few months attending all the courses I could. I went to briefings, seminars and symposiums to find out what was going on in the big wide world, culminating one week before I handed in my uniform with an attendance at a final Resettlement briefing. This was to be conducted by a young officer from the Education Corps, supposedly specially trained in resettlement issues. The briefing was due to start at 1200 hours on a Wednesday and I, like the good soldier I was, turned up several minutes before time. As soon as I arrived I was hurried in to see this officer.

'OK', he started as I sat down. 'Any questions for me? I'm sorry this is going to be a bit rushed but I have to play rugby this afternoon and I'm running a bit late.'

Notes

1. Senior boy soldiers were allowed to have motor scooters or motor-bikes if they were old enough to own them legally.

2. In boy service we had all ranks up to Apprentice or Junior Warrant Officer Class Two (College Sergeant Major). Each squadron or company was lead by a boy service sergeant, supported by two corporals and each barrack room was supervised by a lance corporal.

3. Each night we had a Men's Service SNCO on duty within the accommodation and it was his job to check that all personnel were accounted for, that the barrack room lights were turned off at the appointed hour and that all remained quiet and secure until reveille next morning.

4. Every third weekend was a compulsory hobbies weekend, where boys took part in such varied activities as canoeing and canoe building, rock climbing, social services (helping out at the local psychiatric hospital), pot-holing, attending the Scout troop, and camping/hill walking. Every Wednesday was compulsory hobbies evening and the boys would either partake in the same hobbies as at the weekends, if time and logistics permitted, or an alternative activity such as stamp collecting, chess and even magic classes.

5. If the individual to be crucified was heavy, two broom handles would be used.

6. I returned to this unit 19 years later as the RSM and the lads were still living in the same accommodation.

7. In some countries the UK government has an agreement with the host nation that servicemen and women will be handed over to the military authorities for all crimes committed on their territory. Exceptions to this are capital offences such as murder. In some

instances you will get caught by both military and civilian authorities for the one offence, for example, drink driving may mean that you are fined and lose your licence under civil law and then receive a military penalty as well.

8. Non-tradesman means that you are regarded as without any trade at all. You are simply a person with a service number, who appears on a unit nominal roll and who is entitled to the very basic rate of pay. You would have passed recruit training but either not attended or failed Special to Arms training.

9. Although totally illegal, some units ran a voluntary fines scheme to finance such functions as farewell presentations, parties, minibuses and other such schemes. If a soldier rebelled against the voluntary fine he would stand a very good chance of having formal disciplinary action taken against him and the outcome would be guaranteed to exceed the voluntary fine.

10. Close Observation Patrol. These patrols spend extended periods in hiding, usually in rural areas watching suspects.

11. Usually a private soldier who acts as a butler for the officer. He washes, irons and cleans their uniforms and does numerous other menial tasks such as fetching tea, coffee, posting mail, etc. He cleans the officer's car and acts as stable lad if the officer has a horse.

12. All over the southern part of this country locals keep honey bees and it is easy to buy pots of the nectar.

13. The Royal Engineers or, to use the correct title, 'the Corps of Royal Engineers' is manned by personnel who, no matter what their rank, should be properly referred to as 'The Gentlemen of the Corps of Royal Engineers'. A tradition which I'm led to believe goes back to the days when the corps was made up solely of officers.

14. Aide-de-camp. A middle-ranking officer who acts as personal assistant to a senior officer.

15. Nuclear, Chemical and Biological Warfare.

16. Queen Alexandra's Royal Army Nursing Corps.

17. These were almost exclusively ex-servicemen who looked after the quarters and should have had some understanding for the hassle and problems associated with military married quarters. If they did, not many ever showed any empathy with the occupants.

18. British Army on the Rhine or plainly the British Army contin-

gent in what was occupied West Germany. We were confined to the northern half, with the US Army in the much pleasanter and far more scenic south and Bavaria. Other NATO forces would be scattered across the country.

19. If you owned a car registered with the BAOR authorities, you were entitled to buy petrol coupons that could be exchanged at filling stations for discounted fuel. Your engine size dictated the amount of coupons issued each month and, of course, it was illegal but not unknown for personnel to sell these to other military personnel.

20. In military circles the word 'materiel' (spelt as shown) means all the materials and equipment that make up a specific unit or sub-unit; e.g., in an armoured regiment their materiel would include their tanks, uniforms, radios, etc. For a command post, it would include such items as tentage, tables, chairs, boards, heaters, radios and stationery.

21. Special Investigations Branch. Part of the Royal Military Police (now part of the Adjutant Generals Corps) and equivalent to the CID of a normal civilian police force.

22. The Provost Marshal is the senior military police officer of the garrison or district.

23. Staff College. There are single service and joint service colleges and junior and senior colleges, set up to teach officers how they should be doing the job and to prepare them for future promotion. They are attended by all services and by many from friendly allied nations (in the past that included Argentina, Iran and Iraq).

24. The respective Army or Corps Directorate produced the scripts for each demonstration. They very rarely changed from one year to the next and the only people who had copies were the units concerned with that particular demonstration and a few senior instructors from the Staff College.

25. At that time any senior NCO, warrant officer or commissioned officer charged with drunk driving in Germany (on duty or off) automatically faced a court martial.

26. I was always getting confused between a cook and a chef. What was the difference? We used to have a saying about the cooks: 'Right! Who called the cook a c**t?' Reply was 'Well! Who called the c**t a cook?'

27. This is not the sort of work the guard commander would be able

to authorise on his own and was totally out of character for him as well. In fact he was a bit of a shifty individual himself.

28. For those who are not familiar with this car, the VW Beetle had the engine in the rear compartment.

29. RAATs list such things as assistance to units going on exercises, operational tours, demonstrations such as the Royal Tournament and Edinburgh Tattoo, and other training commitments. They may tell you to provide personnel, equipment, vehicles, or just bed and breakfast, for passing troops. In my time with under strength units and the over-commitment of resources, the RAATs were a thing feared by unit commanders as they could strip some units down to very basic levels. In some cases, this would mean closing your unit down as you had no one left to do any justifiable training or basic tasks.

30. This was the minimum sentence possible under orders from the garrison commander, who had initiated a clampdown on this offence and issued specific punishment levels for those found guilty. Prior to someone appearing before their CO, it is not uncommon for an RSM and/or the unit adjutant to discuss disciplinary actions with the commanding officer. A limited amount of plea-bargaining would be allowed and mitigating circumstances would also be reviewed. Although it was against regulations for a CO to see the soldiers' Conduct Sheets prior to announcing sentence, it would be unusual for the officer not to have some prior knowledge of the man's background.

31. Garrison Messes by their very nature have members from an assortment of cap-badges and even from different services.

32. A subsequent blood test would show that his estimated blood alcohol level at the time of the incident was in excess of 450mg/100ml (maximum legal driving limit in the UK at the time was 80mg/100ml), more than sufficient to put most people into a coma or to kill them.

33. As is common with most messes all the rooms are of similar design and decorated to a standard MoD colour scheme.

34. No disciplinary action was taken against the other person.

35. In military terms this is equivalent to driving without insurance.

36. This referred to the vehicle and the tree he hit.

37. Section 69 of the Army Act 1955. A really useful disciplinary section that encompasses all and everything.

38. Military tradition requires that the accused be escorted by at least one other soldier (of equal rank or, when possible, at least one rank superior). I think this is in case the accused attacks the officer, who would obviously be unable to defend himself.

39. Another weird tradition is that the officer hearing the case should not have access to the soldier's military records until after he finds the accused guilty and just before he announces sentence. He can then read the soldier's conduct sheets and if necessary have the soldier's immediate superior officer (usually his company commander) act as his defence counsel and state any mitigating circumstances.

40. MFO boxes are wooden tea chest type containers. MFO stands for Married Families Overseas and the boxes were used, originally, for the freighting of family possessions between overseas postings.

41. Medical Reception Station, much like a small hospital with small wards, pharmacy, basic treatment facilities, etc. In some cases, the MRS and unit medical centre would be co-located.

42. The Provost Sergeant acts like the unit senior policeman, is in charge of enforcing discipline and running the unit guardroom and jail. In many units he is the nearest thing to Neanderthal man and someone that is not employable in any other job. Usually appears to have the social and man-management skills of someone trained by the Kray twins.

43. A pace stick is a wooden object carried by RSMs and drill sergeants and is used to check the length of a matching soldier's stride or pace. It is also used for measuring distances and for poking soldiers when they need to be poked.

44. A Garrison Sergeant Major (GSM) is a Warrant Officer Class One usually, but not always, on extended service and is based at the Garrison HQ. His job is garrison-level ceremonial duties, Presiding Member of the Garrison Sergeants' Mess, adviser to unit RSMs when required and he acts as RSM for the HQ staff. He can also have various other responsibilities such as control of garrison sports facilities and playing fields, overseer of security at garrison churches, liaison with civil police forces, and he can be chairperson of the garrison road safety committee and a variety of other tasks to fill his day.

45. Artificer Sergeant Major (ASM) is the senior Warrant rank in the Corps of the Royal Electrical and Mechanical Engineers and is usually in charge of a major workshop. A Regimental Corporal Major (RCM) can be found in such units as the Household Cavalry Regiment. Tradition has it that is they do not have any sergeants in these units as the origin of the word 'sergeant' meant servant.

46. Regimental Quartermaster Sergeant. Usually the second most senior Warrant Officer in a unit.

47. I was to slightly alter my name and be an employee of the Forestry Commission working in the Forest of Dean, hoping to hell that no one would know too much about the intricacies or activities of such employment.

48. The reason I wore my watch on the right wrist was that at the time I used to do a lot of free-fall parachuting and wore a wrist-mounted altimeter on the left arm.

49. Messes are run by a committee, which is lead by the PMC or President of the Mess Committee. However, the senior Mess member acts as Presiding Member and effectively rules the Mess. In the case of the Regimental Sergeants' Mess this is usually the RSM or the senior warrant officer on establishment.

50. I believe this goes back to the days when the then Prince of Wales (later King Edward VIII) was aboard a Royal Navy ship but when he stood for the Loyal Toast he hit his head on a bulkhead.

51. In later life this man left the Forces after 20-odd years' service and became a chronic alcoholic. Living under a cardboard box in a public park he became one of the many lost souls so common amongst ex-servicemen. When he died the only personal possession found with him was a pewter statue of a British Paratrooper. Along with many of his ex-comrades I attended his funeral at which his favourite rock-and-roll tunes were played.

52.'Crap hats' was the term used by Paras to affectionately describe anyone was not Airborne (or Special Forces) and thus did not wear the famous 'Red Beret'. Anyone wearing the Red Beret who did not parachute was known as a 'Penguin' (a bird that did not fly).

53. We had to attend and pass Unit Pre-Parachute Selection before progressing on to Centralised Pre-Parachute Selection. If you passed this you could attempt All Arms Parachute Selection or 'P' Company,

as it was affectionately known.

54. CQMS (Company Quartermaster Sergeant): depending on the size of the formation this appointment could either be a Staff Sergeant or Warrant Officer Class Two. In regiments or battalions each squadron or company would have such an appointment (hence either SQMS or CQMS) and the appointee would usually be a staff sergeant answering to the regimental quartermaster (QM) and regimental quartermaster sergeant (RQMS). In smaller independent units the appointee would usually be a Warrant Officer Class Two, who would answer direct to the QM, as the unit would not justify an RQMS.

55. Unbeknown to us, and for his own safety, he had been posted out of his last unit while under investigation for a sexual attack on a fellow cook.

56. On such occasions the police had to concede that, with or without their assistance, such activities would be carried out. It was therefore sound logic for them to be on the side of safety and sensibility, and to carry out one of their prime functions, which is to safeguard life and property.

57. Most of our training jumps were done carrying our normal battle equipment, i.e. 60lb bergen, rifles, webbing, and any other specialist equipment such as mortars, radios, stretchers, machine guns, etc. A clean fatigue jump was just that, no equipment at all, other than the main and reserve parachutes of course, and were nicknamed 'Dolly Lobes' or 'Jollies'.

58. The leader of each load of parachutists is known as the Stick Commander, and it his responsibility to carry out the mandatory safety checks and warn each person about their duty to carry out the parachute descent when ordered. The warning went something like this, 'The green light constitutes a warning order to parachute. The red light constitutes a direct order to parachute. Failure to carry out this order may lead to a court martial.'

59. Nearly all military parachute jumps, worldwide, are done using static-line rigs that automatically deploy the parachute as you fall away from the aircraft.

60. A little known fact of English military history is that until August 1918 either hand could be used to salute with. Before this date Army Orders decreed that the hand furthest from the person saluted was

used and after this date regulations stated that only the right hand be used.

61. Hearts and Minds was a way for gaining field intelligence. You used to treat the locals for illnesses or injury while asking questions about personnel movements, activities around their village, or other such things.

62. Second lieutenants are young inexperienced officers just starting out on their military careers. They have been brainwashed into believing that they have all the necessary qualifications to lead men. The truth is that they know very little indeed of the way the real Army works. Having been told to initially rely upon the experienced SNCOs who will look after them for the first few years, they still charge into situations that they cannot handle. Commonly referred to as 'one-pipped wonders'.

63. Army ration packs come in boxes, which contain all you need for one day. Most soldiers open them and remove the items they do not like such as the hard dry biscuits, jam, toilet paper, powdered soup, etc. This usually halves the weight you have to carry.

64. We intended to remain in the aircraft after the trainees had been dispatched and with the aircraft doing one quick circuit of the DZ we would carry out a free-fall descent from 6000ft, all ten of us exiting from the same door.

65. This is supposed to be one man out every second but usually it is a touch faster and results in paratroopers colliding in the slipstream behind the aircraft or two, or more, Paras getting entangled with each other.

66. So for some reason the British Airborne are trained and dispatched by the Royal Air Force. In almost all other countries I visited it was the Army that did this and in some the dispatcher would follow out the last man as he actually belonged to the unit or formation that was parachuting on that task.

67. Supplies were delivered once a fortnight and would consist of fresh water, Army ration packs, ammunition (if needed), radio batteries, medical supplies, clothing, and any other equipment needed including personal mail occasionally. We also received a small quantity of fresh meat, bread and eggs. These had to be eaten the same day they arrived, as we had no way of storing them. Nor did we want wild

pigs or other animals getting to them before we could savour their delights. The smell of the meat would also attract an abundance of insects.

68. Pole beds were made using an 'A' frame at both ends and poles inserted along sleeves on either side of a hammock. This made a fairly rigid bed over which a poncho could be made into a roof. Mosquito nets could also he hung from the frame to protect the occupant. It was usual for one end of the bed to be secured to a tree and this would give it more strength and stability.

69. In the jungle at night, we used to change out of the clothes we wore during the day as they would be wet and sweaty, and put on our spare dry clothes and boots. Next morning it was always a treat to take off your dry warm kit and put back on the cold damp uniforms we wore each day. A soldier who slept in anything other than some type of uniform would be no good if he were called into action during the night. This rule applied to all theatres of war.

70. R & R: Rest and Recuperation. A chance to relax, do some sight-seeing, meet the locals, and prepare for the return back to base.

71. These courses were held several times a year, therefore the weather could be rather unpredictable. Some mornings at this time it would be fairly warm but on others it could be raining or even have snow on the ground. This was part of the effect required and the students' reactions were closely monitored.

72. Returned to Unit. That is to say they had failed the selection course and were returned to their parent unit.

73. The café was owned by an ex-policeman who allowed us to specially adapt the sound system to do this and as the messages were in a form of covert veiled speech, the other customers would not understand the messages or think that they were part of a routine emergency service's radio call that the system had picked up.

74. At this time the Army scale of equipment for certain units, or appointments within units, meant that not all personnel were issued with a personal weapon when they went off to war, for example, only a certain proportion of medical personnel were issued weapons.

75. The unit used to receive twice-monthly intelligence updates but to get fresh and accurate reports we watched satellite TV and could find out what was going on within hours, if not minutes, of anything

happening.

76. While out of the front line and back in a base area on a spot of R & R, we had watched as a famed and very well-known reporter did a TV news article stating that she was out in the desert close to the front line, when she was in fact in the car park of the five-star hotel. That evening we watched the report broadcast on TV and were highly impressed by the whole deception.

77. No sooner had we covered over the pits than the locals appeared and dug them up again.

78. During this campaign, as with most other recent conflicts that the British Army has been ordered to, national newspapers have instigated crusades to send the humble poor soldier small parcels of goodies to help cheer him up. These are very successful and thousands of parcels are dispatched by well meaning-people, much to the heartfelt thanks of the recipients.

79. This was in the days before GPS systems became available to the British Army.

80. These were, and still are, much prized items in British Army ration packs.

81. Firqas: groups of defected enemy fighters now sworn to fight for the Sultan. The enemy were called 'Adoo'.

82. MRE means Meals Ready to Eat. These were the basic combat rations for North American Forces and were similar to the twenty-four- hour Composite (Compo) rations packs issued to the British.

83. Nuclear, biological and chemical suits. These consisted of a jacket with hood, trousers, two pairs of gloves (inner and outer) and over boots, plus your respirator. There were various other items such a Nerve Agent Protection System tablets (NAPS) and atropine auto-jet injections.

84. Queen Alexandra's Royal Army Nursing Corps.

85. After many months of applying for Redress of Grievance against the award, the soldier was able to recover this money.

86. One of the problems in a situation like this is that personnel are not normally required to notify the unit if they go away for the weekend. So you may find some of them have gone up in the mountains, sailing offshore, visiting the continent, or just off visiting relatives.

87. Obviously smoking during such patrols is not allowed, for two reasons. One that it is not tactical and, secondly, nicotine affects the blood supply to the rods and cones in the back of the eye and reduces one's ability to see in low light situations.

88. Territorial Army and Volunteer Reserve.

89. Depending on the type of unit, training weekends could be held two or three times a month.

90. Drill Nights are training evenings which most, if not all, of the unit is expected to attend. Each detachment or HQ would have one Drill Night per week. If you have several detachments these might be on the same night or different, depending on how many PSIs you have.

91. DOWO means District Ordnance Warrant Officer and is/was the supreme RQMS of the respective military district.

92. Each corps, arm or service has a commander on the staff of the District or Area Headquarters and they act as the next highest authority for that branch.

93. Depending on the size of the unit and the rank of its commander, you were allowed to write off 'Small Stores Losses'. This may be up to a limit of several hundreds or even thousands of pounds without any formal higher authority. The unit commander has to sign each form stating that he is happy that no disciplinary matters have been involved and that he has investigated each loss. He can, however, sign one, two or ten forms each day as long as none exceeds the laid down limit. It is very rare for anyone to question these write-offs unless they become totally outlandish.

94. The QM wanted half the PSIs in uniform and half in civilian clothing. This would have meant the ones in civilians walking around the town centre with pistols stuck in their pockets or down the backs of their trousers, etc.

95. Transfers In (TFIs) were usually, if officers, someone that was destined not to make it in their own corps or regiment. In this case the chap was a commissioned former regular Army RSM, which would be taken as an indication that he was not considered suitable officer material in his own unit and that the only way for him to gain a commission was to move to another arm/service.